W9-AJQ-129

Other *For Better or For Worse*® Collections

Retrospectives

Little Books

A *For Better or For Worse*® Collection by Lynn Johnston

**Andrews McMeel
Publishing**

Kansas City

www.FBorFW.com

03 04 05 06 07 BBG 10 9 8 7 6 5 4 3 2 1

ISBN: 0-7407-3412-1

Library of Congress Control Number: 2002111034

―――――― **ATTENTION: SCHOOLS AND BUSINESSES** ――――――

Andrews McMeel books are available at quantity discounts with bulk purchase for educational, business, or sales promotional use. For information, please write to: Special Sales Department, Andrews McMeel Publishing, 4520 Main Street, Kansas City, Missouri 64111.

Long before the car accident that brought Michael Patterson and Deanna Sobinski together, they had been classmates, third-grade sweethearts, and now, after years apart, different pathways, different lives, they were together again—talking about marriage.

Having grown up in a family where marriage meant security, Michael was keen to tie the knot. He had, surprisingly, few reservations about going down the aisle, making serious promises, and planning a life with someone else. Every thought he had he said out loud. Deanna held his heart in her pocket. Deanna, on the other hand, saw ceremonial marriage as a farce. A wedding was a trip to fairyland, an expensive one, which meant little to her, perhaps because it meant so much to her mother.

Mira Sobinski had never been a "bride." Not in the contemporary sense. Hurriedly married by a priest in a dockside chapel, she and her husband, Wilfred, climbed the gangplank onto a vessel bound for Halifax, Nova Scotia. Their only possessions were in two thick fabric bags, their futures uncertain. Wilfred could speak a little English. He and Mira were bound for Canada; Poland would soon be left far behind. A new country terrified him and excited her. Wilfred joined family members in a hardware business in Milborough, Ontario, where they prospered. Two daughters were born and Mira saw that they had everything.

MICHAEL, WHEN YOU FIRST MET ME, I WAS ENGAGED. MY MOTHER HAD EVERYTHING PLANNED A YEAR IN ADVANCE.

SHE KNEW WHAT KIND OF CEREMONY IT WOULD BE, WHAT KIND OF FLOWERS, WHAT KIND OF CAKE...

THEN, THERE WAS THE DRESS, THE BRIDE'S MAIDS, THE MUSIC, THE FOOD, GIFTS FOR THE WEDDING PARTY, TABLE DECOR, RECEPTION DINNER...

WHAT ABOUT THE GROOM?!!

MICHAEL, AT THAT POINT, HE COULD HAVE BEEN ANYBODY!

When it came, finally, to arranging a wedding for the Sobinskis' elder daughter, Andrea, Deanna saw her sister crumble under the stress. Mira wanted perfection. Mira wanted to put on a show—forgetting completely the needs and desires of the people who were marrying! Andrea and her fiancé eloped, leaving Mira confused and angry, and causing a serious rift in the family.

Deanna was in her first year of university when a young man she had been dating proposed to her. He was a kind person, attractive and polite. He worked for her father and his name was Perry. Deanna, unsure of her feelings, asked him to wait, but her mother begged her to accept his ring. "Love takes time," she told her daughter. "Things you don't like about him now, you can change later." Deanna accepted his proposal and in an instant, both young people became actors in a complex play—written, produced, and directed by her mother. Deanna knew she couldn't play this role. Marriage was for life! But breaking an engagement meant breaking a heart. Repeatedly, she deferred the date of the wedding.

When Deanna met Michael again, she told him she was engaged, that a relationship would be impossible. Still, she couldn't get the smiling young man, the writer, the one with the sense of humor, out of her mind. She broke her engagement to Perry and began to see Michael Patterson. Michael felt he had "won." Eternally optimistic and living in the world of a storyteller, he fabricated a future for them both, not knowing that every overture, every suggestion of permanence made her shy away from him. He was perplexed by the rejection. This wasn't in the script. After all, Deanna loved him; he knew it. He could see it in her face, in her mannerisms, and in the way she would "bump into" him at university—when their classes were on opposite sides of the campus. It took awhile for him to convince her he was for real, no matter what. All he wanted to know was, would she make a commitment to him, and if not, why not?

Guilt. It pulls you down mentally and physically until you push to the surface, and with the help of others, breathe again. Deanna felt guilty about her sister's elopement, about her own broken engagement, about the growing contempt she had for her mother—and about the way she was treating Michael. They had been dating steadily and both were about to graduate: she with a degree in pharmacy and he as a journalist.

Despite the many opportunities she had to tell Michael how much he meant to her, she couldn't quite manage to say "I love you." It was too definite a statement, a message too clear. She had once told someone else she loved him. Was it because he wanted to hear the words or was it from the heart? Or was it because her mother wanted to plan a wedding, a grand extravagant wedding. A wedding Mira always wanted for herself?

It was New Year's Eve. Gordon Mayes's small apartment was filled with friends. He and Tracey were the first of "the group" to marry. Young and freshly out of high school, they made their home in a small space above the automotive garage where Gordon had worked as a student and now owned, thanks to the generosity of his boss and a substantial loan from Michael's father. Potluck dishes covered the small kitchen table. There was little room to dance, but the party rocked, spilling out onto the back porch with whistles and singing and shouts of "Happy New Year!" Michael climbed onto the roof and shouted into the night, "I LOVE DEANNA SOBINSKI!" She begged him to get down. "Not until you say you love me," he said and turned to shout again, "Michael Patterson is crazy about Deanna Sobinski!" The words were swept into the night. Michael was wearing just a light sweater. The roof was icy and the wind was strong. He was about to shout again when Deanna—in front of friends who had gathered on the porch behind her, shouted back to him, "I love you!" She said it. The words came easily. It was like passing the hardest exam and getting the highest grade. It felt absolutely wonderful.

It *was* a New Year. Everything was new. Michael had already started to make a name for himself as a writer and Deanna's career as a pharmacist lead her first to accept locum work, taking over when full-time drugstore staff went on holiday. She enjoyed the variety, she liked the freedom, and best of all, she was not making a commitment. A full-time commitment of any kind was still something Deanna could not imagine. She thought about her parents, the arguments and capitulations, the nagging and the games, the frequent days of silence. Was this what marriage meant?

Loving a man was one thing; marrying him was another. How long could she sustain the love without agreeing to marriage? She needed time to think, to clear her mind, to get away. Deanna joined a medical missions team and left Canada to work in Honduras for six months. Michael was devastated. For the first time, he could imagine himself really losing her—to illness, an accident perhaps, or even to another man. His imagination worked overtime. He said good-bye at the airport. And then he waited.

Deanna returned a different person. The things she had seen and done made life in North America seem gluttonous and spoiled. She'd seen real loss and real poverty and she realized, in comparison, how unimportant her problems were. Now, in Michael's embrace she felt confident. If she could secure a full-time job, she said, she would marry him.

There was no "proposal." There was simply a joyful understanding between two people in love that they could make a life together—but when? An opportunity to replace a pharmacist taking maternity leave at the Hospital for Sick Children in Toronto promised to provide Deanna full-time work. People frequently left the lab for vacation or were moved to other areas. There would soon be no excuse to vacillate. And perhaps now . . . she didn't need one.

Michael moved from the apartment he shared with his photographer friend "Weed" to a rented house in Toronto. It seemed crazy, he thought, to have all this space to himself. He asked Deanna to move in with him. Despite her need for freedom, the thought of common-law living didn't appeal.

They were engaged. Together, they bought the ring, a diamond solitaire set in white and yellow gold. They announced their engagement to both families. Michael's parents were delighted to welcome Deanna and said so, with a candlelit dinner and champagne. Deanna's father shook Michael's hand firmly, enjoying the thought of having a son to talk to, and Mira Sobinski immediately began planning the great event.

Her list resembled preparations for a royal visit, and was divided into several columns: GROOM, GROOM'S FAMILY, GROOMSMEN, BEST MAN, ATTENDANTS. Under each heading was a long list of essentials. The flowers

included the rehearsal dinner, corsages, boutonnieres, bouquets, chapel decorations, centerpieces, and a going-away arrangement. Color schemes for each pre- and post-occasion were carefully coordinated, as suggested by *Your Ultimate Perfect Day*—a wedding bible that left no detail unaddressed.

The dress. Nothing was more important than the dress! After all, the bride's appearance would set the ambiance for the entire occasion! Mira bought four thick magazines: *Bride to Be*, *Bridal Brilliance*, *Magnificent Bride*, and the ever-popular *Elegant Weddings,* which Deanna dubbed *EW* for short. Mira absorbed them all. From these, she selected numerous potential dresses and pasted a photocopy of her daughter's graduation portrait over the face of the model in each gown. Deanna's response was to burst into tears, which Mira took to be inexpressible gratitude for the work she had done. Overwhelmed and unprepared, Deanna promised to choose a dress, as her mother's list lengthened.

The columns BRIDE and BUDGET filled two pages in fine print. The line marked TOTAL EXPENSES remained blank. Wilfred Sobinski said nothing. He cleared his mind and prepared for a visit to his accountant. Deanna moaned. Why couldn't they just have a small intimate wedding? How could she make everyone happy?

"Can you keep a secret?" she asked Michael. Her plan was simple. Get married now. Michael had interviewed a local pastor and felt comfortable asking her to perform the ceremony. "Then it will just be us," Deanna said "It will mean more to me, and we can save the fanfare for the family!"

11

Close friends Gordon and Tracey Mayes were asked to be their witnesses, and despite the simplicity and the short notice, Michael and Deanna's secret wedding was moving and meaningful. They exchanged rings with emotion and sincerity, and their promises said without an audience meant more than a broadcast on CNN.

Mrs. Michael Patterson moved into Michael's rented house, much to the chagrin of Deanna's mother, who, not knowing they were already wed, thought her behavior was disgraceful. John and Elly Patterson accepted their decision without criticism. Michael had told only his parents about the secret wedding, and he knew they were people he could trust. Meanwhile, Mira's machine was in full gear.

SEE, THE PROBLEM WITH BEING A PROFESSIONAL PHOTOGRAPHER IS THAT FRIENDS ALWAYS WANT YOU TO TAKE THEIR WEDDING PHOTOS!

SO, YOU END UP TAKING ORDERS, STRUGGLING WITH KIDS, ORGANIZING RELATIVES, GETTING THOSE "CANDID" SHOTS OF THE HAPPY COUPLE— AND WORKING...

WHILE EVERYONE ELSE PARTIES ON!!!

SO, WHO DO YOU SUGGEST WE ASK, WEED?

ME....

....I'D WANT YOU TO HAVE THE BEST.

Few amendments to her plans were made. Josef Weeder, now a photographer in great demand, offered to do the wedding photos as a gift. Mira agreed. Mira allowed the floral arrangements to be provided by Mike's childhood friend, Lawrence Poirier, from Lakeshore Landscaping. Caterers were called, invitations designed, announcements were worded. Michael and Deanna kept their wedding rings hidden in a bedroom drawer and appeared at Mira's functions with grace and good humor. A wedding shower and several dinners for the groom were organized. Mira saw to it that all the right people were invited, and despite their resentment, the objects of her affliction had to admit that Mira had gone to a lot of effort on their behalf.

I TOLD YOU MY MOTHER WOULD DRIVE US CRAZY!

PEW BOWS! WE'RE NOT GETTING MARRIED 'TIL SEPTEMBER, AND ALREADY, SHE'S NATTERING ABOUT PEW BOWS!

DO WE EVEN WANT PEW BOWS?

YES....

AND THEY HAVE TO MATCH MY BOUQUET AND THE BRIDE'S MAID'S DRESSES.

BRIDE'S MAIDS?

YOUR SISTERS, MY FRIEND, JUDY AND MY SISTER WILL BE MATRON OF HONOR. YOU GET TO CHOOSE 2 GROOMSMEN AND THE BEST MAN.

OH....

WELL, I'VE LEARNED ONE THING ABOUT THIS, DEANNA. IF TWO PEOPLE CAN SURVIVE 8 MONTHS OF WEDDING PREPARATIONS.... THEY CAN SURVIVE ANYTHING!

13

It was easy for Deanna to say "I love you" now. Her husband and future groom allowed himself to be fitted for the suit his mother-in-law chose for him. He cheerfully approved the menu, the guest list, and the wine. He drank beer with his father-in-law and talked about hardware. He met their neighbors, relatives, and friends. Michael Patterson was everything Mira could ever have wanted in a husband for her daughter. He was honorable, came from a nice family, was gainfully employed, and looked particularly good in gray.

As Mira checked off her list of wedding requirements, the bride checked off the days on her calendar. Tensions mounted and so did the bills. Countdown. Deanna wondered why her father had given her mother carte blanche to host a wedding they could hardly afford.

Sometimes it takes an outsider to see through windows fogged by years of misunderstandings, jammed shut by silence. Wilfred Sobinski loved his wife, and as much as she wished this grand celebration for her daughter, he wished it for Mira. This wedding was for her, a girl who'd worn a torn woolen coat over a soiled cotton dress and married a man she hardly knew because he could speak a little English and would take her to a better place, she hoped.

Michael Patterson saw Deanna's family through different eyes, perhaps it was because a writer likes to analyze things or perhaps his own upbringing gave him such insight. Love, he thought, is undefinable. It comes and goes and whatever it is, real love binds people together in sickness and in health, for richer for poorer, for better or for worse.

A ceremony doesn't make a marriage. Commitment does. Sincere commitment, mutual respect, the willingness to compromise, and a good sense of humor. That's what his father had told him, and Michael now knew it was true.

WOW! LOOK AT THAT!!!

YOU KNOW, ELLY— I LOVE THIS TIME OF YEAR!

REALLY?

UH HUH. I ALWAYS LOOK FORWARD TO FEBRUARY THE 15TH.

HONEY, VALENTINE'S DAY IS ON THE 14TH!

I KNOW.

THEN, WHAT'S SO WONDERFUL ABOUT THE 15TH?

...CHOCOLATE GOES FOR HALF PRICE!

LYNN

WELL, THANKS FOR TELLING ME, DAD. 'BYE...

WHAT'S UP, LIZ?

MY GRANDFATHER HAD A HEART ATTACK. NOT A MAJOR ONE, BUT IT WAS ENOUGH TO SCARE EVERYBODY!

WHAT WAS HE DOING, READING "PLAYBOY"?

NO...

HE WAS ON HIS WAY TO THE CORNER STORE TO BUY CIGARETTES.

DON'T DO IT, OK LIZ?... DON'T LECTURE ME ABOUT SMOKING.

I'M NOT!

I JUST SAID MY GRANDFATHER WAS ON HIS WAY TO BUY CIGARETTES WHEN HE HAD A HEART ATTACK.

RIGHT.

AND, HE'S ALMOST 80, RIGHT? I FIGURE IF YOU CAN SMOKE AND LIVE THAT LONG, WHAT MORE DO YOU WANT?

—TO LIVE TO BE 81?

KNOW WHAT, LIZ...YOU NON-SMOKER FREAKS BITE ME! YOU PIOUS KNOW-IT-ALLS WITH ABSOLUTELY **NO** VICES OF YOUR OWN...

IT'S NONE OF YOUR BUSINESS IF I WANT TO LIGHT UP. THIS IS MY BODY, MY CHOICE, MY HABIT. IT'S WHAT I WANT TO DO.

I DON'T SMOKE INSIDE. I DON'T LEAVE MY BUTTS AROUND. I DON'T DO ANYTHING TO INTERFERE WITH YOUR PERSONAL AIR SPACE. SO, BACK RIGHT OFF. —AM I GETTING THROUGH?

YOU'RE RIGHT, CANDACE. I APOLOGIZE. I'M SORRY THAT I CARE.

YOU'RE SORRY THAT YOU CARE?!! — WHAT KIND OF ✱◎⚡ APOLOGY IS THAT?!!

I DON'T WANNA SEE YOU DIE YOUNG!

EVERYBODY DIES, LIZ. YOU GOTTA DIE OF SOMETHING! — IF I CHOOSE TO CROAK WITH A PACK IN MY POCKET, THEN, WHAT'S IT TO YOU?

BESIDES, I LIKE SMOKING. IT GIVES ME PLEASURE. THIS LITTLE ROLL OF PAPER IS MY SUPPORT SYSTEM, IT'S MY BUDDY — MY PAL'!

I CAN UNDERSTAND THAT.

I JUST HOPE YOUR BUDDY DOESN'T LET YOU DOWN.

HEY, CANDACE!

HEY YOURSELF.

WHAT'S EATING YOU?

TELL ELIZABETH TO KEEP HER OPINIONS TO HERSELF.

WHAT ARE YOU TALKING ABOUT?

OH, YOU'LL FIND OUT. WAIT 'TIL SHE FINDS SOMETHING ABOUT YOU SHE DOESN'T APPROVE OF, AND YOU'LL GET A SERMON FROM THE PREACHER.

HEY, NO PROBLEM!

THERE'S NOTHING ABOUT ME NOT TO LIKE!!!

I SAW CANDACE OUTSIDE — SHE WAS PRETTY MAD!

YEAH. I GOT ON HER CASE ABOUT SMOKING.

YOU CAN'T CHANGE PEOPLE, LIZ. YOU'VE GOT TO ACCEPT THEM AS THEY ARE — BAD HABITS AND ALL!

SO, DO I HAVE ANY BAD HABITS THAT YOU'VE LEARNED TO ACCEPT, ERIC?

NO BAD HABITS...

— YOU'RE JUST NOT BAD ENOUGH!!

17

HOO! I JUST GOT AN E-MAIL FROM MY SISTER. SHE AND HER ROOM MATE ARE NOT GETTING ALONG SO WELL!

ROOM MATES! MAN, AM I GLAD THOSE DAYS ARE OVER! I MEAN, WEED'S A GREAT GUY AN' ALL, BUT HE DID THINGS THAT MADE ME CRAZY!

HE HAD THIS HABIT OF TAPPING HIS FINGERS ON THE TABLE. HE ALWAYS CHEWED GUM WITH HIS MOUTH OPEN, AND.....

WHAT?

THIS IS THE THIRD CUP OF HALF-FINISHED COFFEE I'VE FOUND! -WHY CAN'T YOU FINISH A CUP OF COFFEE?!

—LYNN

DEANNA, I'M SORRY ABOUT THE COFFEE. I'VE ALWAYS LEFT HALF-FINISHED CUPS AROUND. I JUST FORGET WHERE I PUT THEM, AND...

MICHAEL, YOU ALSO LEAVE THE TOOTHPASTE OUT AND YOU PUT STUFF IN THE DISHWASHER, WITHOUT RINSING IT!

WAIT A MINUTE!

SUDDENLY IT'S "FIND A FAULT" WEEK?

NO, I JUST WANTED TO MENTION A COUPLE OF THINGS YOU DID THAT WERE BOTHERING ME.

REALLY? -THERE'S MORE?

...I MADE A LIST.

YOU MADE A LIST OF THINGS I DO THAT IRRITATE YOU?!

IT'S A SHORT LIST!

YOU DON'T PUT YOUR SOCKS IN THE HAMPER, YOU DON'T PUT AWAY THE TOASTER, YOU KEEP PUTTING THE NAIL SCISSORS IN THE "SHAVING" DRAWER...

DEANNA, THOSE ARE ALL INSIGNIFICANT QUIRKS AND HABITS THAT AREN'T WORTH WORRYING ABOUT! I DON'T HASSLE YOU ABOUT THE STUFF YOU DO!!

ME? -WHAT DO I DO?

YOU HASSLE ME ABOUT INSIGNIFICANT QUIRKS AND HABITS THAT ARE NOT WORTH WORRYING ABOUT.

—LYNN

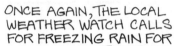
ONCE AGAIN, THE LOCAL WEATHER WATCH CALLS FOR FREEZING RAIN FOR THE NEXT 24 HOURS...

MOM, REMEMBER THAT PLASTIC RAINCOAT GRANDMA CARRIE SENT YOU?

UH-HUH.

COULD I PLEASE BORROW IT?

SURE, HONEY!

IT'S A BIT LONG.

THAT'S OK.—I CAN MANAGE!

WELL, ISN'T THAT SOMETHING!— IT'S FREEZING RAIN AND APRIL IS WEARING A RAINCOAT!!

FINALLY. SOME GOOD, OLD COMMON SENSE HAS CREPT INTO HER HEAD!

3-4

HI, MRS PATTERSON. HOW'S YOUR DAD?

HE'S FINE, LAWRENCE. —THANKS FOR ASKING!

MIKE CALLED ME WHEN IT HAPPENED. SORRY I WASN'T HERE.

YOU SENT A CARD. THAT WAS THOUGHTFUL!

SPEAKING OF THOUGHTFUL, I LIKE WHAT YOU'RE DOING WITH THIS PLACE! I LIKE THE NEW COLORS, THE ENTRANCE, THE SHELVES, THE CHOICE OF STOCK.... I THINK YOU'RE MANAGING EVERYTHING SO WELL!!

...I GUESS STORE OWNERS DON'T GET ENOUGH COMPLIMENTS, DO THEY!

IT'S GOOD TO SEE YOU, LAWRENCE! CAN I HELP YOU WITH SOMETHING?

SURE CAN!

I NEED A GIFT FOR A FRIEND'S NIECE, WHO'S TURNING 3.

LET'S LOOK OVER HERE.

"HELP DIGBY DUCK FIND HIS QUACK!"—THIS LOOKS COOL. IT GIVES YOU EVERY BIRD AND ANIMAL SOUND IMAGINABLE!

UM... THAT MIGHT BE A BIT ANNOYING.

GREAT! —THAT MEANS SHE'LL **LOVE** IT !!!

MY FRIEND, NICHOLAS AND I ARE GOING TO HIS NIECE'S THIRD BIRTHDAY PARTY— AND I CAN'T WAIT!

I'LL PROBABLY NEVER HAVE KIDS OF MY OWN—SO I REALLY ENJOY LITTLE JEN.

WHO'S NICHOLAS?

HE'S A DESIGNER. WE MET AT SCHOOL, AND HE'S BEEN HELPING ME AT LAKE-SHORE LANDSCAPING.

WELL?...IS THERE ANYTHING "BETWEEN" YOU TWO?

YES... BUT I'M AFRAID TO DISCUSS THIS WITH ANYONE YET.

YOU CAN CONFIDE IN ME.

WE'RE TALKING ABOUT FORMING A PARTNERSHIP... AND TAKING OVER THE BUSINESS !!

LAKESHORE LANDSCAPING IS SOLID, MRS. P. IF I HAVE A PARTNER, WE COULD BUY IT OUT.

I WANT TO TAKE OVER THE PLACE, MAKE THE REAL DECISIONS- HECK, I'VE BEEN DOING ALL THE WORK FOR 2 YEARS ANYWAY!

YOU KNOW WHAT I'M SAYING!-WHAT'S THE DIFFERENCE BETWEEN MANAGING A BUSINESS AND OWNING ONE?

ONE CAN BE A MILESTONE AND THE OTHER CAN BE A MILLSTONE.

THE PEOPLE WHO STARTED THIS COMPANY 30 YEARS AGO, ARE READY TO RETIRE.

NICK AND I THINK WE CAN MAKE THEM A GOOD OFFER, BECOME PART OWNERS AND BUY OUT THEIR SHARE OVER A PERIOD OF TIME!

SOUNDS GOOD, LAWRENCE, BUT A VENTURE LIKE THIS MEANS THAT YOU AND NICK HAVE TO REALLY TRUST EACH OTHER. A BUSINESS PARTNERSHIP IS NOT UNLIKE A MARRIAGE!

I KNOW.

WE'RE READY TO MAKE THAT COMMITMENT.

LAWRENCE CAME INTO THE STORE TODAY, CONNIE

HE'S LOOKING GOOD, ISN'T HE, EL.

EVER SINCE HIS FRIEND, NICHOLAS STARTED WORKING WITH HIM, HE'S BEEN SO FOCUSED AND FULL OF SELF CONFIDENCE.

DO YOU MIND IF I ASK WHAT THEIR RELATIONSHIP IS?

ELLY, I DON'T PRY INTO MY SON'S PERSONAL LIFE. AS LONG AS HE'S HAPPY AND PRODUCTIVE-THAT'S ALL THAT MATTERS!

RIGHT...

...MY ADULT KIDS DON'T TELL ME EVERYTHING THEY'RE UP TO, EITHER!

HOW DID THE SHOPPING GO?

I TRIED ON EVERY DRESS IN THIS ONE STORE, MIKE. EVERY SINGLE DRESS!

AND YOU FOUND NOTHING YOU LIKED?

THERE'S A DESIGN BY ROMONA KEVEZA THAT'S PERFECT.

GOOD! YOU HAVE YOUR WEDDING DRESS, THEN!

MAYBE.

WHAT DO YOU MEAN, "MAYBE"?

MOM WANTS TO CHANGE THE COLOR, THE FABRIC, THE NECKLINE, THE SKIRT AND THE VEIL.

I NEVER THOUGHT SHOPPING FOR THIS DRESS WOULD BE SO HARD, MICHAEL!

I WANT MY MOM TO BE HAPPY, BUT OUR TASTES ARE SO DIFFERENT!

PART OF ME SAYS "THIS IS **HER** DAY NOW, LET HER MAKE ALL THE DECISIONS"....

BUT, THE OTHER PART OF ME DOESN'T WANT TO WALK DOWN THE AISLE, LOOKING LIKE A CHANDELIER!

MAYBE YOU COULD DO IT IF YOU WERE "LIT"?

AFTER WE LOOKED AT DRESSES, WE CHOSE STATIONERY AND GIFTS FOR THE ATTENDANTS

MY MOM WANTS THE INVITATIONS TO BE GOLD EMBOSSED ON SCENTED VELLUM WITH MATCHING RSVP CARDS.

SHE WANTS FAVORS AT EVERY PLACE SETTING, THAT'S 250 AND A THREE TIERED CAKE WITH....

STOP!

DOES SHE HAVE ANY IDEA HOW MUCH THIS WILL COST?!!

ABOUT $50,000.⁰⁰

WHAT?

MAN, IF THE VOWS DON'T BIND US, THE GUILT WILL!!

BEEBADEEBA DEEBADEEBA DEEEP!!!

YACK YACK YACK YACK YAP YAP

YAP YACK YAP...

WELL, I'LL CALL YOU LATER, BOB! OK! CIAO!

DINGALINGALINGA LINGALINGGG!

HEY! WHAT'S UP? ME? OH, NOTHING, JUST SITTING IN A QUIET, EXPENSIVE RESTAURANT TRYING TO HAVE A ROMANTIC EVENING WITH MY WIFE...

WHAT?!! SURE, NO PROBLEM— HE'S RIGHT HERE!!!

....IT'S FOR YOU.

EVER SINCE DEANNA AND HER MOM GOT FULL SWING INTO THIS WEDDING STUFF, IT'S ALL SHE EVER TALKS ABOUT!

WE CAN'T WALK DOWNTOWN ANYMORE WITHOUT LOOKING AT FABRICS, MENUS, TABLE DECORATIONS, CANDLES AND CLOTHES!

AT LEAST I DON'T HAVE TO WORRY. ALL I'VE GOTTA DO IS GO SOMEPLACE AND RENT A TUX!

MOM WANTS YOU IN DARK STEEL GREY, WITH PINSTRIPED VEST, MATCHING TIE AND ORCHID.

Lynn

MICHAEL, DO YOU LIKE MY HAIR LIKE THIS?

SURE!

WHAT IF I CURLED IT!!

SURE!

WHATEVER YOU WANT!

SHOULD I CUT THE FRONT A BIT?

YOU DON'T REALLY CARE ABOUT MY HAIR, DO YOU?!!

ALL I CARE ABOUT IS THE CUTE FACE THAT'S UNDER IT!

I CAN'T EVEN SAY SOMETHING ROMANTIC AND I'M IN TROUBLE!!!

Lynn

SEARCH, SHUFFLE, POKE, SEARCH, RUMMAGE

AAAGH!!

MICHAEL, THIS WEDDING BUSINESS IS DRIVING ME NUTS!

I KNOW! RELAX!

TAKE IT EASY DEANNA!

PROMISE ME I'LL NEVER HAVE TO GO THROUGH THIS AGAIN!!!

Lynn

29

IT'S GONNA BE YOUR BIRTHDAY SOON, ISN'T IT, GRAMPA!

YES.... I'LL BE 80 YEARS YOUNG.

LIZ AN' MICHAEL AN' UNCLE PHIL AN' AUNT GEORGIA WILL BE HERE – AND MOM'S MAKING YOUR FAVORITE SUPPER!

SOUNDS LOVELY.

AND THEN, IT WILL BE YOUR BIRTHDAY JUST A FEW DAYS LATER!

I LOVE BIRTH-DAYS, DON'T YOU?

LET'S JUST SAY I'M GRATEFUL, NOW FOR EVERY ONE!

Lynn

IT'S MY DAD'S 80TH BIRTH-DAY TOMORROW, CONNIE. HE'S BEEN SO SENTI-MENTAL, LATELY.

HE DOESN'T WANT A BIG CELEBRATION, JUST FAMILY... BUT, HE HAS INVITED A LADY HE'S BEEN SEEING LATELY.

YOUR DAD HAS A GIRL-FRIEND?

HE CALLS HER HIS DANCE PARTNER. EVERY WEDNES-DAY NIGHT, THEY MEET AT THE LEGION, AND THEY DANCE.

HOW DO YOU FEEL ABOUT THAT?

IT'S MUSIC TO MY EARS!

Lynn

77, 78

79...

80!!

HAPPY BIRTHDAY TOOO YOUUU HAPPY BIRTHDAY TOOO YOUUU HAPPY BIRTHDAY DEAR GRAND

PAAAAAGH!!

Lynn

PLEASE, MOM? PLEASE CAN I HAVE A SLEEPOVER? IT'S GONNA BE MY 10TH BIRTHDAY! I'M 2 DIGITS, NOW!!!

I ONLY WANNA INVITE 6 GIRLS

6 IS QUITE A FEW.

WELL, BECKY WON'T COME IF I DON'T ASK FAITH, AN' FAITH IS BEST FRIENDS WITH MELIA WHO WON'T COME IF I DON'T ASK CHANTAL AN' CHANTAL HANGS OUT WITH JEWEL AN' ASHLEIGH ..... SO, THEY ALL HAFTA COME!

WHY DO THEY "ALL HAFTA COME"?

BECAUSE, I ALREADY ASKED BECKY!

WAS THAT A YES?!!! OH, COOL!!- I CAN HAVE A SLEEPOVER!

BECKY? IT'S OK! EVERYONE CAN COME! COUNTING ME, THERE'S GONNA BE 7 HERE FOR MY BIRTHDAY!!!

WE'RE GONNA HAVE GAMES AN' PIZZA AN' RENT MOVIES AN' STAY UP ALL NIGHT !!

WHOA!

EVERYTHING ELSE IS FINE- BUT YOU ARE **NOT** STAYING UP ALL NIGHT!

≳TSK≲ SHE IS SOOooooo MEAN!!!

ELLY, YOU JUST HAD A BIG BIRTHDAY PARTY FOR YOUR DAD- ARE YOU SURE YOU DON'T MIND ANOTHER PARTY IN THE HOUSE?

APRIL REALLY WANTS A SLEEPOVER, JOHN.

BUT 7 KIDS!

IT'LL KEEP US AWAKE UNTIL MIDNIGHT!

THAT'S OK.... SOME DAY, SHE'LL BE KEEPING US AWAKE UNTIL MIDNIGHT....

....AND, WE WON'T KNOW WHERE SHE IS.

IT'S ONE O'CLOCK IN THE MORNING! — WHY DO THEY CALL THIS A **SLEEP** OVER?

BECAUSE, WE GET TO SLEEP WHEN IT'S OVER!!

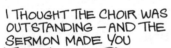

THAT WAS A LOVELY SERVICE, WASN'T IT, JOHN.

IT SURE WAS.

I THOUGHT THE CHOIR WAS OUTSTANDING — AND THE SERMON MADE YOU THINK!

TODAY ISN'T ABOUT EGG HUNTS AND CHOCOLATES AND BIG FAMILY SUPPERS....

IT'S ABOUT RENEWAL, BEING GRATEFUL, IT'S ABOUT CARING DEEPLY FOR ONE'S FELLOW MAN.

YES, I MUST ADMIT THAT WAS ONE OF THE MOST REFRESHING EASTER SERVICES I'VE EVER ATTENDED!

BUT, GRAMPA! — YOU SLEPT THROUGH THE WHOLE DARNED THING!!!

Lynn

40

SO, THIS IS MY NEW HOVEL.

LOOKS GOOD, WEED!

TOOK ME A WHILE TO FIND IT. THE RENTS IN THIS BURG ARE BRUTAL!

I LOVE THESE OLD HOUSES, JO—THEY HAVE SUCH CHARACTER!

YEAH...

CHARACTER BEING ANOTHER WORD FOR "NOTHING WORKS"

YOU TWO LOOK GOOD! COHABITATION WORKS, DOES IT?

SO FAR, WE'RE STILL TOGETHER!

HOW ARE THE WEDDING PLANS? IS EVERYTHING STILL ON FOR SEPTEMBER FIFTEENTH?

OH, MAN.

WHAT DID I SAY?!!

THE WORD "WEDDING".—IT'S TAKEN ON A WHOLE NEW MEANING.

YOU MEAN "'TIL DEATH DO WE PART" ISN'T BAD ENOUGH?!!

DEANNA'S MOM WANTS TO SPEND $50,000°° ON OUR WEDDING, WEED.

HOOOO...

FOR THOSE CLAMS, YOU COULD PUT A DOWN-PAYMENT ON A HOUSE!

OR BUY A CAR THAT WORKS.

BUT THIS IS WHAT SHE'S ALWAYS WANTED, AND SHE'S SPARING NO EXPENSE.

SHE'S SPARING NO FEELINGS EITHER, I SEE.

41

43

IT WAS SPUR OF THE MOMENT! A FRIEND WHO'S A MINISTER MARRIED US— WITH GORD AN' TRACEY AS WITNESSES

THEY'VE KEPT THE SECRET WELL.

IT HAS TO BE KEPT A SECRET. IF MY MOM FINDS OUT...

WE KNOW.

I'VE ALWAYS BEEN HONEST WITH YOU. I COULDN'T KEEP THIS FROM YOU ANY LONGER!

MOM? DAD?— PLEASE ...SAY SOMETHING!!!

CONGRATULATIONS

WOW. I AM SO RELIEVED! I THOUGHT YOU'D BE ANGRY OR INSULTED OR...

WEDDINGS ARE AS PERSONAL AS BIRTH AND DEATH, SON. EVERYONE MUST OBSERVE THESE LIFE-CHANGING EXPERIENCES IN THEIR OWN WAY.

AN EXTRAVIGANT WEDDING IS RIGHT FOR SOME PEOPLE, AND TOO MUCH FOR OTHERS.

SHOULD WE CANCEL THE BIG ONE IN SEPTEMBER THEN?

ARE YOU CRAZY? ... I BOUGHT A DRESS !!!!

SO, OUR MICHAEL IS A MARRIED MAN. HARD TO BELIEVE, ISN'T IT.

I KNOW THEY'RE NOT HAPPY WITH DEANNA'S MOM... BUT, I'M GLAD THEY'RE HAVING A BIG WEDDING IN SEPTEMBER.

I WANT TO SEE HER WALK DOWN THE AISLE. I WANT TO HEAR THEM TAKE THEIR VOWS. I WANT THE FLOWERS AND THE PHOTOS.

AND, THE TEARS?

...THEY CAN COME NOW.

PAT PAT PAT

Z Z Z

...I LIKE MY COUCH WARMED!

SORRY, DAD - I FORGOT TO TELL YOU. THERE WAS AN E-MAIL FROM YOUR BROTHER WISHING YOU A HAPPY BIRTHDAY! - I PRINTED IT OUT!

WELL, WELL. I DIDN'T KNOW ERNIE COULD WORK A COMPUTER! LOOK AT THIS... AN ACTUAL E-MAIL.

LONG MESSAGE, TOO! ...ALL ABOUT HIS FAMILY. NICE MESSAGE FOR MY 80TH! - SAYS A LOT MORE THAN ONE OF THOSE STORE BOUGHT CARDS!

... I WONDER WHY IT MEANS A LITTLE LESS!

OK... I TURN ON THE MACHINE AND I WAIT FOR THE LITTLE PICTURES TO LINE UP ALONG THE BOTTOM OF THE SCREEN....

NOW I SELECT THIS LITTLE DOODLE HERE, AND IT TAKES ME TO THE E-MAIL PLACE AND THEN... I DO WHAT?

*Ø✕❋◉ DARNED ✳ THING!!

NO WONDER THEY CALL THAT LITTLE FLASHING LINE THERE, A "CURSER".

46

SCOOP!

TRASH

HEY, MOM, CAN I HAVE THE CAR?

SURE!

I'M TAKING YOUR RED COAT, IS THAT OK?

UH HUH.

WHERE ARE THE KEYS?!!

IN THE POCKET!

Row 1

"I LIE AWAKE AT NIGHT, IRIS...AND I TALK TO MARIAN."

"I LIE AWAKE AND TALK TO GEORGE."

"I'VE TOLD HER THAT NOBODY WILL EVER REPLACE HER, BUT..."

"I'VE TOLD GEORGE ABOUT YOU, TOO"

"WHEN HE WAS IN THE HOSPITAL, HE TOLD ME TO GO ON WITH MY LIFE...THAT AFTER HE DIED I WOULD LOVE AGAIN."

"WE LOST GOOD PARTNERS, DIDN'T WE."

"MAYBE IT'S POSSIBLE TO FIND GOOD PARTNERS AGAIN."

Row 2

"I LIKE YOUR FAMILY, JIM. IT'S SO NICE THAT YOU CAN LIVE WITH THEM."

"YES. I'VE BEEN BLESSED."

"BUT, I'VE STARTED TO THINK ABOUT GETTING A LITTLE PLACE OF MY OWN."

"GO ON! NOT REALLY!"

"I'M SECURE ENOUGH NOW, I THINK I'M READY TO LIVE ALONE AGAIN."

"YES... IT WOULD BE NICE TO HAVE THE INDEPENDANCE"

"...IT WOULD BE NICE TO HAVE THE PRIVACY!"

Row 3

"WELL, HERE WE ARE AT YOUR APARTMENT BUILDING."

"I ENJOYED THE WALK, JIM. THANK YOU."

"WOULD YOU LIKE TO COME UP FOR A MINUTE OR TWO?"

"A MINUTE OR TWO WOULD BE FINE!"

"IT'S LATE. YOUR DAUGHTER WON'T WONDER WHERE YOU ARE?"

"IRIS, LET'S PRETEND WE'RE THE COUPLE IN THE MOVIE WE JUST SAW..."

"...AND KEEP EVERYONE GUESSING!"

WELL, MIKE - IT'S SURE GONNA BE GREAT WHEN YOU TWO HAVE KIDS OF YOUR OWN!

IT ISN'T JUST MENO-PAUSE THAT'S KEEPING ME AWAKE, JOHN— IT'S OTHER STUFF!

FLAP FLAP

MY DAD ISN'T HOME YET AND IT'S AFTER MIDNIGHT, MIKE AND DEANNA ARE BEING PUSHED INTO AN EXPENSIVE WEDDING THEY DON'T WANT...

AND, I CAN'T GET RID OF THE WEIGHT I'VE GAINED!—I'M SO OLD AND FAT! LOOK AT ME! DON'T I LOOK OLD AND FAT?!!

SNOZZZZZZ

I'VE HEARD THAT WHEN SOME ANIMALS ARE IN SERIOUS DANGER... THEY "PLAY DEAD."

LYNN

WHERE COULD MY FATHER BE? JUST LOOK AT THE TIME!

SOY MILK

MAYBE HE RAN FOR A TAXI, AND.... NO, IF HE WAS IN THE HOSPITAL, SOMEONE WOULD HAVE CALLED

HE TOOK IRIS TO A MOVIE... BUT WHAT WOULD THEY BE DOING AT THIS TIME OF NIGHT?

...NAHHH...

LYNN

GOOD MORNING, MY DEAR!

DAD! THANK HEAVENS! I WORRIED ABOUT YOU ALL NIGHT!— WHERE IN THE WORLD WERE YOU?!!

WELL, AFTER THE MOVIE, IRIS INVITED ME UP TO HER APARTMENT.—I GUESS I FELL ASLEEP ON HER SOFA, SO SHE COVERED ME UP AND WE CALLED A CAB IN THE MORNING.

I AM SO RELIEVED! I THOUGHT IT MIGHT BE YOUR HEART!

YOU DON'T HAVE TO WORRY ABOUT MY HEART, DEAR...

I'VE GIVEN IT TO IRIS.

LYNN

WOW! SO MICHAEL AND DEANNA ARE MARRIED! —HOW DO YOU FEEL ABOUT THAT?

A LITTLE EMPTY. A LITTLE SAD.

YOU'RE ANGRY BECAUSE THEY DIDN'T TELL YOU.

SURE... BUT I UNDERSTAND WHY.

HEY, YOU'RE A MOTHER-IN-LAW, NOW, EL! YOU CAN TELL THEM HOW YOU FEEL!—SAY WHAT'S ON YOUR MIND!

I THINK I'D RATHER BE THE KIND OF MOM-IN-LAW WHO KEEPS HER MOUTH SHUT!

LET ME GET THIS STRAIGHT: DEANNA'S MOTHER IS SPENDING A FORTUNE ON AN ENORMOUS WEDDING AND DOESN'T KNOW THAT THE KIDS ARE ALREADY MARRIED.

BINGO.

WHAT IF THE NEWS "LEAKS OUT"?

SO FAR, THE ONLY PEOPLE WHO KNOW ARE JOHN, ME, GORDON, TRACEY, JOSEF WEEDER AND NOW, YOU.

NONE OF US IS GOING TO TELL, RIGHT?

RIGHT!

BUT THE JUICIER THE SECRET, THE HARDER IT IS TO KEEP!

THERE'S ANOTHER THING BOTHERING ME, CONNIE. ELIZABETH IS GOING TO STAY UP NORTH THIS SUMMER.

SHE ALREADY HAS A JOB!

THEY HAVE TO LEAVE HOME SOMETIME, EL!

THAT'S NOT ALL...

HER ROOM MATE IS GOING TO LIVE WITH HER AUNT AND LIZ CAN'T AFFORD TO PAY RENT HERSELF...

I'M AFRAID SHE'LL MOVE IN WITH HER BOY FRIEND!

SHE HAS TO MAKE HER OWN DECISIONS

BUT, I WANT HER TO MAKE THE RIGHT ONES!!

HAS ELIZABETH ACTUALLY SAID SHE'S MOVING IN WITH HER BOYFRIEND?

NO, BUT THE OPPORTUNITY IS THERE

AND IF DEANNA'S MOTHER FINDS OUT THAT THE KIDS GOT MARRIED IN SECRET, I DON'T KNOW WHAT WILL HAPPEN—SHES GOING TO ALL THIS EXPENSE AND...

ELLY, THESE ARE NOT INSURMOUNTABLE PROBLEMS! WHY ARE YOU MAKING YOURSELF CRAZY?!!

... I'VE GOT TO DO **SOMETHING!**

I GUESS YOU NEVER STOP WORRYING ABOUT YOUR KIDS, CONNIE...

CRICK!

APRIL!

HI, MOM

I THOUGHT YOU WERE OUTSIDE!

HOW LONG HAVE YOU BEEN SITTING THERE?

UMMM

HAVE YOU BEEN LISTENING INTO OUR CONVERSATION?!!!

WELL...

I LISTENED TO SOME OF IT.

WHAT DID YOU HEAR?!

UHHH

PROBABLY ALL THE STUFF I WASN'T SUPPOSED TO.

APRIL, TELL ME WHAT YOU HEARD.

I HEARD YOU TELL CONNIE THAT MICHAEL AN' DEANNA WERE MARRIED ALREADY

'AN YOU'RE SCARED LIZ MIGHT MOVE IN WITH ERIC.

OOOHHH

I'M SORRY, MOM—I DIDN'T MEAN TO LISTEN! I WON'T SAY ANYTHING TO ANYONE—I PROMISE!

I CAN KEEP A SECRET AS WELL AS **YOU** CAN!!!

OHHHH... I AM SO GLAD TO BE HOME !!

PEEL PEEL PEEL PEEL

MRS. NEDWITT DIDN'T SHOW UP FOR A THREE HOUR APPOINTMENT THIS MORNING, SO WE JUGGLED PATIENTS, TRYING TO FILL THE SPACE....

THEN, OUR COMPUTER AT THE FRONT DESK WENT DOWN, SO WE WERE OUT OF COMMISSION FOR MOST OF THE DAY.

I MISSED LUNCH....

WE HAVE TWO STERILIZERS AND ONE STOPPED WORKING. THEN, THE SUCTION SYSTEM PACKED UP. THERE WAS ENOUGH TENSION AMONG THE STAFF I THOUGHT THE PLACE WOULD EXPLODE!

MELVISS DRIVEL LEFT HER WHINY KIDS IN THE RECEPTION AREA WHILE WE DID HER CLEANING AND ONE OF THEM BROKE A LAMP....

MY DENTAL CHAIR LOCKED INTO THE "DOWN" POSITION, SO I SPENT ALL AFTERNOON WORKING IN A POSITION LIKE THIS!!

HOW WAS YOUR DAY?

FINE!

... I WAS GOING TO TELL HIM IT WAS TERRIBLE!!

Lynn

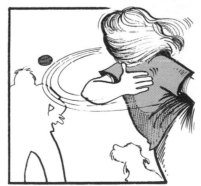

58

MOM? APRIL KNOWS, DOESN'T SHE.

SHE OVERHEARD ME TALKING TO CONNIE.

CONNIE KNOWS? SO DOES GRANDPA.

WE'LL BE DEAD MEAT IF MIRA SOBINSKI FINDS OUT THAT DEE AND I ARE MARRIED!

THE SLIGHTEST LOOK, THE MOST INNOCENT REMARK COULD GIVE IT AWAY!

DON'T FRET, SON - YOU CAN COUNT ON US!

NUDGE, NUDGE, WINK-WINK, EH?...NUDGE NUDGE, WINK-WINK!

WHAT'S EVERYONE TALKING ABOUT SO QUIETLY IN HERE?

NOTHING, MIRA. WE'RE JUST HELPING WITH DESSERT.

I SENSE SOME SECRECY. WHAT IS GOING ON?!

OK, MOM - I'LL TELL YOU.

DEANNA, WAIT!

I'VE CHOSEN MY WEDDING DRESS.

WITHOUT ME?!

SOMETIMES YOU HAVE TO LIGHT A SMALL FIRE IN ORDER TO PREVENT A BIG ONE!

DEANNA! HOW COULD YOU CHOOSE A DRESS? - I SHOULD HAVE BEEN CONSULTED! AFTER ALL, WHO'S PAYING FOR IT?!

I AM!

I FOUND ONE I LIKED AND I PUT A DEPOSIT ON IT.

BUT

MIRA, I CALLED THE FLOWER SHOP, THE CATERER AND THE BAND.

EVERYTHING CAN BE CHANGED, MOM. WE DON'T WANT YOU TO SPEND A FORTUNE!

BUT, I WANT IT TO BE MARVELLOUS!

AND I WANT IT TO BE **ME**!!

Panel 1: I'M SO UPSET! HOW COULD YOU GO BEHIND MY BACK AND CHANGE ALL MY PLANS?! / WE DIDN'T CHANGE ANYTHING!

Panel 2: WE JUST ASKED IF THEY COULD BE CHANGED! WE WANT THINGS TO BE SIMPLE! DEANNA AND I ARE NOT EXTRAVIGANT PEOPLE! / ARE YOU CALLING ME EXTRAVIGANT?!!!

Panel 3: MIRA, IF THE KIDS WANT TO SAVE US MONEY... / WILFRED, STAY OUT OF THIS!

Panel 4: MOM, IF THESE PEOPLE ARE OUR RELATIVES, NOW... I HOPE THEY'RE OUR ONLY "SHOUTING ONES".

Panel 5: EXCUSE ME. I'M JUST AN OLD VETERAN — BUT I'D RESPECTFULLY LIKE TO INTERRUPT THIS DISCUSSION.

Panel 6: RIGHT NOW, AT THIS MOMENT, PEOPLE ARE FIGHTING OVER FOOD, SHELTER, MEDICINE — AND A SAFE PLACE TO RAISE THEIR CHILDREN.

Panel 7: AND, HERE YOU ARE — FIGHTING OVER THE COST OF A WEDDING.

Panel 8: NOW THAT, MY FRIENDS — IS LUXURY.

Panel 9: GOOD NIGHT.

Panel 10: GRAMPA? CAN I COME IN? / YES, DEAR. I'M NOT SLEEPY.

Panel 11: IS YOUR MOTHER ANGRY WITH ME FOR SAYING MY PEACE? / NOPE. THE SOBINSKIS APOLOGIZED AN' EVERYONE'S GONE HOME

Panel 12: GRAMPA — WE KEPT MIKE AN' DEANNA'S SECRET, DIDN'T WE! / WE DID, INDEED.

Panel 13: THERE'S A TIME FOR OPENING YOUR MOUTH, APRIL... AND A TIME FOR KEEPING IT SHUT!

Panel 14: ...THE TRICK IS TO KNOW WHEN TO DO WHICH!

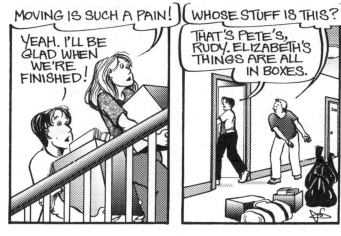

HEY, RUDY.
HEY, LIZ.

I DIDN'T KNOW YOU WERE MOVING INTO PETE'S ROOM.
YEAH. I BOUGHT HIS BED FRAME AN' BOX SPRING.

I THOUGHT YOU WERE MOVING IN WITH ERIC!
I AM, BUT EVERYONE NEEDS THEIR OWN SPACE!
SO, KNOCK IF YOU'RE COMIN' INTO MY ROOM—OK?

ERIC, YOU DIDN'T TELL ME THAT RUDY WAS STAYING IN THE APARTMENT!
YEAH—ONLY PETE MOVED OUT.

BUT IT'S JUST A TWO BEDROOM PLACE!
AN' RUDY SLEEPS IN THE LIVING ROOM!

WHAT ABOUT PRIVACY?
NO PROBLEM.

THE ONLY ROOM THAT'S NOT REALLY SOUND PROOF IS THE BATHROOM.

ERIC, WHEN WE TALKED ABOUT MOVING IN TOGETHER, I THOUGHT IT WOULD BE JUST US!

HEY, YOU NEVER SAID YOU WANTED A WHOLE ROOM TO YOURSELF! BESIDES, WHAT AM I S'POSED TO DO—THROW RUDY OUT?

AND THIS WAY, WE SPLIT THE RENT 3 WAYS! YOU'LL BE PAYING NEXT TO NOTHING!

...AND LIVING NEXT TO ME!

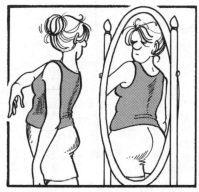

AAGH! I CAN'T STAND MY BODY! I BULGE OUT EVERYWHERE!

LOOK AT ME! I USED TO HAVE SUCH A NICE, FLAT TUMMY!

I HAD NICE LEGS, TOO.

I TRY TO EAT RIGHT! I TRY TO EXERCISE! I DO EVERYTHING I CAN TO RETAIN MY FIGURE!!

I WISH SOMETHING COULD BE DONE TO MAKE ME FEEL BETTER ABOUT THE WAY I LOOK!!

HEY, UGLY BROTHER! WELL, I DID IT. — I MOVED IN WITH ERIC.

OUR APARTMENT'S IN AN OLD BUILDING WITH NO ELEVATOR OR AIR CONDITIONING, BUT THE KITCHEN'S OK AND I HAVE MY OWN ROOM.

I BOUGHT A BED FRAME, BOX SPRING AND OTHER STUFF FROM THE GUY WHO MOVED OUT, SO I ACTUALLY OWN SOME FURNITURE!

FOR THE FIRST TIME IN MY LIFE, I FEEL LIKE AN ADULT!!

ERIC, PETE LEFT A BUNCH OF BEER CASES UNDER THE BED. COULD YOU HELP ME GET RID OF THEM?

NOT REALLY.

THE MIDDLE SUPPORT IS BROKEN, SO THE BEER CASES ARE WHAT'S HOLDING IT UP.

HE NEVER SAID IT WAS BROKEN!

HEY! 50 BUCKS, LIZ... YOU GOT A BARGOON!

YEAH, THIS HERE IS YOUR GENUINE "BOX SPRING"!

I BOUGHT A BROKEN BED!

COME ON, LIZ. YOU'RE NOT GONNA SLEEP IN IT ANYWAY!

ERIC, I MAY BE LIVING WITH YOU NOW, BUT I WANT MY OWN SPACE — AND THAT MEANS HAVING A BED I CAN USE!

HEY, I WAS JUST MAKING A COMMENT! EVERYONE DOES THEIR OWN THING AROUND HERE!

EVERYONE'S TOTALLY EQUAL.

UH, LIZ?...

— CAN YOU MEND SOCKS?

SOMETHING WRONG, LIZ?

NO. I WAS JUST THINKING ABOUT WHAT A SERIOUS STEP THIS IS.

A SERIOUS STEP?

MOVING IN WITH YOU! IT'S A MAJOR COMMITMENT. I JUST WANT IT TO WORK OUT!

ELIZABETH, WHAT WE HAVE TOGETHER IS MAGIC! YOU ARE THE MOST IMPORTANT THING IN MY LIFE. TRUST ME. THIS WILL WORK OUT.

AN' HEY! — IF IT DOESN'T... WE'LL MOVE ON!

WHATCHA GOT THERE?

MIXING BOWLS, TEA TOWELS — SOME OF THE KITCHEN STUFF WE'RE MISSING.

HOT ROO

I ALSO BOUGHT A MATTRESS AND SOME CURTAINS FOR MY ROOM!

IT'S AMAZING WHAT YOU CAN FIND IN THE SECOND HAND STORES! I EVEN GOT 4 PLACEMATS FOR 3 BUCKS!

PLACEMATS? WHY DO WE NEED PLACEMATS?

THEY'RE FOR RUDY TO PUT HIS ELBOWS ON WHILE HE'S EATING CEREAL OUT OF THE BOX.

SOGGIES

ROAD HAWG

ERIC, I DON'T WANT TO SOUND MEAN OR ANYTHING, BUT COULDN'T RUDY FIND ANOTHER APARTMENT?

GIVE HIM A CHANCE, LIZ. HE'S A GOOD GUY.

DON'T YOU THINK THIS ARRANGEMENT IS ... AWKWARD?

SLIME KOMIX

I MEAN — WE'RE A "COUPLE", NOW. IT'S LIKE HAVING SOMEONE ELSE LIVING IN OUR PLACE!

JUST THINK OF HIM AS SUB-LETTING!

SNIFF, SNORT, URBPP!

I THINK OF HIM AS SUB HUMAN!

IS EVERYONE READY?

SURE!

YEP!

AHEM.....

DAD, GRAMPA - BECAUSE YOU MEAN SO MUCH TO US, WE WROTE DOWN SOME OF THE THINGS WE'VE WANTED TO SAY .... AND, MAYBE NEVER TOLD YOU.

THANK YOU FOR ALWAYS BEING THERE FOR US, FOR GIVING US GOOD ADVICE AND FOR LETTING US MAKE MISTAKES WITHOUT CRITICISM.

THANK YOU FOR BEING SUPPORTIVE, EVEN WHEN YOU DIDN'T AGREE WITH OUR DECISIONS.

THANK YOU FOR BELIEVING IN US, FOR DISCIPLINING US FAIRLY AND FOR LOVING US UNCONDITIONALLY.

THANK YOU FOR YOUR SENSE OF HUMOR, YOUR SENSE OF HONOR AND YOUR SENSE OF FUN.

WE WANT YOU TO KNOW THAT WE'RE LUCKY TO BE YOUR KIDS!!! - HAPPY FATHERS' DAY!

WELL, THANK YOU!

YES. THAT WAS WONDERFUL!

JUST WHEN YOU THINK YOU HAVE EVERYTHING - THEY GIVE YOU SOMETHING YOU REALLY NEED!

LYNN

YOU DID WHAT?!!

SO YOU MOVED IN WITH ERIC. WELL, I'M GLAD YOU TOLD ME, HONEY.

WHAT KIND OF STUPID MOVE WAS THAT?!!

YOU'RE AN ADULT, NOW. YOU HAVE TO MAKE YOUR OWN DECISIONS.

IF HE DOES ANYTHING TO HURT YOU, WE WILL KILL HIM!

WE JUST WANT YOU TO BE HAPPY.

YOU'RE WONDERFUL, MOM! I DIDN'T THINK YOU'D BE SO SUPPORTIVE!

SHE DID IT, JOHN. ELIZABETH MOVED IN WITH ERIC.

SHE SAID SHE WAS GOING TO. IT'S NO SURPRISE.

SHE'S SO YOUNG!

SHE'S 20 YEARS OLD, ELLY. KIDS GROW UP.

I KNOW... BUT I STILL THINK OF HER AS AN INNOCENT LITTLE KID.

?

THE BUBBLE'S IN THE MIDDLE OF THE LEVEL, DAD!

GREAT!

NOW, WE'LL ANCHOR THESE STONES IN PLACE WITH A LITTLE CEMENT.

IF YOU'RE NOT CAREFUL, YOU CAN UNDERBUILD THINGS, APRIL. A SERIOUS MODELLER KNOWS THAT HIS STRUCTURES MUST HAVE A LOT OF TOLERANCE.

...AND SO MUST HIS WIFE!

YOU'RE BRINGING IN MORE ROCKS?

I'M ADDING A MINE SITE TO MY MODEL RAILROAD, EL!

THE TOWN WILL BE HERE, RIGHT? BUT, THE PEOPLE HAVE TO WORK SOMEWHERE!

SO I'LL PUT THE HEAD-FRAME THERE, THE MILL WILL BE THERE AND THAT SPACE WILL BE FOR THE BUNK HOUSES!

I LOVE YOU, HONEY.

WHEN A MAN HAS A HOBBY LIKE THIS... YOU ALWAYS KNOW WHERE HE IS!

YOU'RE A BIG HELP, APRIL! WE WORK WELL TOGETHER.

DADDY...?

BECKY SAYS I'M FAT.

WHAT?! - YOU'RE EXACTLY THE WAY YOU SHOULD BE FOR YOUR AGE!

YOU THINK I'M FAT, DON'T YOU.

I THINK YOU'RE ABSOLUTELY PERFECT!

HOW CAN YOU SAY THE RIGHT THING, AND STILL BE TOTALLY WRONG?

HONEY, YOU'RE 10 YEARS OLD! YOU'RE STARTING TO TURN INTO A WOMAN. YOUR BODY IS CHANGING.

SOON, YOU'RE GOING TO SHOOT UP TALL! ... AND, BEFORE THAT HAPPENS, SOMETIMES YOU GAIN A LITTLE WEIGHT!

NOT BECKY - SHE'S SKINNY.

EVERYONE'S BODY ADJUSTS TO CHANGES IN DIFFERENT WAYS!

I WANNA BE THIN AGAIN!

...DON'T WE ALL.

YOU AND APRIL WERE HAVING QUITE A PRIVATE CHAT OUT THERE!- WHAT WAS THAT ALL ABOUT?

BECKY SAID SHE WAS FAT.

APRIL ISN'T FAT, SHE'S NORMAL!

WELL, SHE'S VERY SELF-CONSCIOUS ABOUT BEING A LITTLE "ROUNDER" THAN SHE USED TO BE.

BUT WE TALKED IT ALL OUT, AND SHE'S FEELING A LOT BETTER ABOUT HERSELF, NOW.

I HATE MY HAIR!

MOM- SHOULD I GET MY HAIR CUT?

IF YOU WANT TO, HONEY!

MAYBE I SHOULD PUT THE SIDES BACK LIKE THIS.

THAT LOOKS NICE.

I HATE MY HAIR!

WELL... WHY DON'T WE GO AND HAVE IT STREAKED.

SERIOUSLY?

WHY NOT?!

CAN I DO IT PURPLE?!!

YEAH, WE CAN STRIP THE COLOR OUT AN' PUT IN PURPLE STREAKS.

CAN I MOM?

IT'S YOUR HAIR.

OK, WE HAVE ROSE VENOM, MAD MAGENTA LOUD LILAC AND MAJOR SHOCK.

MAJOR SHOCK! I WANNA GO FOR MAJOR SHOCK!

AAAH!

HEY, UGLY BROTHER! I TOLD THE FOLKS ABOUT MY NEW PLACE, AND AMAZINGLY, THEY'RE COOL!

I'M GETTING GOOD HOURS AT MEGA-FOOD. THEY'VE GOT ME ON FAST-CHEK, SO I GET LOTS OF WIERDOS...

THEY'RE ALLOWED 1-8 ITEMS, RIGHT? WELL, YOU SHOULD SEE WHAT THEY TRY TO PULL OFF!!...

I'VE GOT 36 ITEMS, AND THERE'S 6 OF US. THAT'S LESS THAN 8 ITEMS PER PERSON!!

FAST-CHEK 1-8 ITEMS ONLY

GOOD EVENING! THANKYOU FOR SHOPPING AT MEGAFOOD!

THANKYOU FOR SHOPPING AT MEGAFOOD! WOULD YOU LIKE SOME HELP WITH YOUR GROCERIES?

GOOD EVENING! THANKYOU FOR SHOPPING AT...

FAST-CHEK 1-8 ITEMS ONLY

GREAT. I GET TO GO ON MY BREAK!

GOOD EVENING! THANKYOU FOR SHOPPING AT MEGAFOOD!

HEY, LIZ! GOT A MINUTE?

CANDACE! - I'M JUST GOING ON MY BREAK. - WANNA COME?

THE SIGN SAYS EMPLOYEES ONLY.

DON'T WORRY. IT'S OK.

WOW. SO THIS IS THE LUNCH ROOM IN ONE OF THE BIGGEST GROCERY STORES IN THE PROVINCE!

RIGHT!

AMAZING, ISN'T IT.

TOTALLY.

HOW'S IT GOING WITH ERIC?
FINE! EXCEPT HIS OTHER ROOM MATE HASN'T LEFT, YET.

HE'S A NICE GUY, BUT HE'S CAMPED IN THE LIVING ROOM, AN' IT'S WIERD HAVING THIS THIRD PERSON AROUND!

WHEN I MOVED IN, I THOUGHT IT WAS GOING TO BE "OUR PLACE"— BUT, EVERYWHERE I LOOK, THERE'S RUDY'S CLOTHES, RUDY'S FOOD— HE'S ON THE PHONE, HE DOESN'T CLEAN UP...
SO...

PRETEND YOU'VE GOT KIDS!

YOU CAME TO SEE ME. ARE YOU ALL RIGHT?
YEAH— I JUST WANTED TO TALK.

I'M THINKING ABOUT QUITTING SCHOOL. MY AUNT NEEDS ME TO WORK IN THE STORE.
BUT, CANDACE! — YOU WERE DOING SO WELL!

I WAS AVERAGE. BESIDES, I'M NOT SURE I WANT TO BE A PSYCHOLOGIST ANY MORE.
WHAT ?!!

— ARE YOU CRAZY ?!

EVERYONE HAS DOUBTS ABOUT THEIR CAREERS, CANDACE. I'M GOING TO TEACHER'S COLLEGE, BUT I DON'T KNOW IF I'LL LIKE TEACHING!

SERIOUSLY? YOU ALWAYS SEEM SO SURE OF YOURSELF!
ME?— I'M THE MOST UNSURE PERSON I KNOW !!

I'M NOT SURE I SHOULD BE LIVING WITH ERIC, OR WORKING HERE. I'M BROKE AND HOMESICK. I LOOK AND SOUND O.K. BUT I'M A REAL MESS !!
EMPLOYEES

WOW. THAT MAKES ME FEEL SO MUCH BETTER!

HEY, LIZ—YOU'RE HOME EARLY!

I GOT A RIDE. I INVITED CANDACE OVER, SO SHE PICKED ME UP AFTER WORK.

SO, THIS IS YOUR NEW PLACE!

LEMME FOLD UP THE COUCH, SO YOU CAN SIT DOWN!

THIS IS RUDY. HE'S JUST HERE 'TIL HE CAN FIND ANOTHER APARTMENT.

REALLY.

...WHERE ARE YOU LOOKING?

ERIC, I THOUGHT YOU WERE GONNA CLEAN UP THE KITCHEN!

I NEVER GOT AROUND TO IT!

THE BEDROOM'S A MESS. HOW CAN YOU FIND ANYTHING?

ALL I NEED TO FIND IS YOU.

NOBODY TOOK OUT THE GARBAGE!

I WORKED TODAY, TOO, YOU KNOW!

ISN'T IT SWEET? THEY'VE JUST MOVED IN TOGETHER, AND ALREADY THEY'RE ACTING LIKE AN OLD MARRIED COUPLE!!

WHY DID YOU INVITE CANDACE OVER?

SHE SHOWED UP AT MEGAFOOD AND WANTED TO TALK.

SHE'S THINKING ABOUT QUITTING SCHOOL.

WHO DOESN'T!? HECK, I TOOK A YEAR OFF.

AND, IT WAS A GREAT YEAR! I GOT MY HEAD STRAIGHTENED OUT, AND NOW I'M IN SCHOOL AGAIN.

WHAT STRAIGHTENED YOU OUT?

MY FOLKS SAID THEY WERE GONNA CUT OFF MY ALLOWANCE.

MY FOLKS SAID AS LONG AS I WAS IN SCHOOL, THEY'D PAY SO MUCH A MONTH TOWARDS RENT AN' FOOD, AN' I HAVE TO MAKE UP THE REST.

YEAH, THE DEAL WITH MY FAMILY IS ABOUT THE SAME...

ELIZABETH, LOOK!

IS RUDY PUTTING THE MOVES ON CANDACE, OR WHAT?

COME ON, RUDY DOESN'T MOVE UNLESS FOOD IS INVOLVED!

WE'RE GOIN' FOR PIZZA, GUYS! - WANNA COME?

RUDY AN' CANDACE ARE REALLY GETTIN' IT ON!

I'D NEVER HAVE PUT THOSE TWO TOGETHER!

THEY'RE BOTH SO TOTALLY WIERD!

MAYBE THEY'RE WIERD IN A COMPATIBLE WAY!

I MEAN, WHO KNOWS WHAT STIMULUS ATTRACTS ONE PERSON TO ANOTHER! IS IT VISUAL? IS IT SCENT? IS IT SOME KIND OF GENETIC PATTERNING?

I THINK WE CAN CROSS OFF VISUAL AND SCENT.

SNIFF?

HI, UGLY BROTHER! GUESS WHAT. REMEMBER CRAZY CANDACE HALLORAN? SHE IS NOW DATING THE GUY WHO IS LIVING AT MY PLACE!!

I'VE NEVER PLAYED CUPID BEFORE, SO THIS MATCH BETWEEN HER AND RUDY IS VERY COOL!

I AM REALLY HOPING THIS RESULTS IN HIM MOVING TO HIS OWN APARTMENT, SO ERIC AND I CAN BE ALONE!

I'M LOOKING FORWARD TO HAVING THE KIND OF RELATIONSHIP THAT YOU AND DEANNA HAVE!

SNAP SNAP!
GULP SLUPP SNAP!
SNAP
SNAP GULP SNORP
SLUPP SNAP
GLP
SNAP!
SNAP
SNARP
SNAP
SNRP
SLUPP
SLUPP SLUPP SLP
SLUBP SLUPPPP
SLPT
GLP
SLP
GULP
SLPP
LICK
MFFF
LICK
SLURBP
GULP
MFFF
LICK
WHY CAN'T YOU JUST DRINK OUT OF A BOWL, LIKE NORMAL DOGS?
LYNN

I'M SORRY I FORGOT ABOUT DINNER, HON. WHEN I GET INTO A STORY I FORGET EVERYTHING!

WELL, IF YOU WANT WHAT'S LEFT OF THE CHICKEN, IT'S IN THE MICRO.

BE RIGHT THERE.

TICK-TICKITY-TAP TAP-TAP-TAP-TIC TICKITY, TICK TAP TAPPITY TICK, TAP TICK....

WHOA! IT'S 10 O'CLOCK ALREADY!

I DIDN'T KNOW IT WAS SO LATE!!

DID YOU EAT?

YEAH... I HAD A PEANUT BUTTER SANDWICH!

MICHAEL, WHEN YOU ARE WORKING, I MIGHT AS WELL NOT BE HERE!

I KNOW. I GET SO IMMERSED IN WHAT I'M DOING...

IT'S LIKE BEING IN A TRANCE. I BECOME THE PEOPLE I'M WRITING ABOUT. I SEE THEIR FACES, I SENSE THEIR FEELINGS—I BECOME PART OF THE STORY!

AND, SOMETIMES... THE STORIES SEEM TO WRITE THEM-SELVES!

REALLY!

...TOO BAD YOU HAVE TO BE THERE WHEN IT HAPPENS!

YOU'RE WORKING TOO HARD, MICHAEL. YOU EDIT THESE HUGE MANU-SCRIPTS, AND THEY STILL EXPECT YOU TO PRODUCE ARTICLES OF YOUR OWN.

WE NEED THE MONEY, DEE.

I'M JUST AFRAID YOU'LL BURN OUT!

I KNOW HOW TO PACE MYSELF. I KNOW WHEN TO QUIT.

WHERE ARE YOU GOING?

—I JUST THOUGHT OF A PARAGRAPH I WANT TO CHANGE!

'BYE HONEY. I'M GOING TO WORK. I START AT 7 THIS MORNING.

OH.

I'LL BE HOME A BIT LATE TONIGHT. I'M GOING TO THE BRIDAL SHOP FOR A FITTING.

OK.

I'VE SET THE ALARM FOR 8. I'LL SEE YOU LATER!

SURE. UH-HUH...

BZZZZ!

UH? WHAH? ...DEANNA, WHERE ARE YOU?!!

...NOBODY TELLS ME ANYTHING!

HAVE YOU GOT YOUR DRESS YET, DEANNA?

I ORDERED A WHITE SUIT. I'M TRYING IT ON TODAY.

PHARMACY

A SUIT? BUT I THOUGHT THIS WAS GOING TO BE A REAL, RITZY WEDDING!

IT'S ALL I COULD AFFORD.

YOU ARE BUYING YOUR OWN DRESS?

MOM DIDN'T LIKE ANYTHING I LIKED SO I WENT AND CHOSE SOMETHING ON MY OWN!

AND WHAT DOES SHE THINK ABOUT THAT?!

I DON'T KNOW. SHE ISN'T SPEAKING TO ME.

IS ANYONE GOING TO THE BRIDAL SHOP WITH YOU, DEE?

MY FIANCÉ'S MOM IS MEETING ME THERE

OOH, I SEE TROUBLE! IF YOUR MOTHER FINDS OUT THERE'LL BE FIREWORKS!

SHE WON'T FIND OUT.

I LEFT MICHAEL A NOTE THIS MORNING. HE KNOWS WHERE I'LL BE, AND HE'S AWARE OF THE SITUATION.

...IF HE TOLD HER, HIS MIND WOULD HAVE TO BE ON ANOTHER PLANET!!!

RRRING!

THE FACE ON MARS

Panel 1: I'M SO GLAD YOU COULD MEET ME HERE, ELLY. I REALLY NEEDED SOMEONE ELSE'S OPINION.

GOWN GALLERY

Panel 2: I SAW THIS ON THE DISCONTINUED RACK. IT WASN'T MY SIZE, SO THEY FOUND ONE AT ANOTHER STORE.

Panel 3: IF I REMOVE THE ROSE AND CHANGE THE BUTTONS, IT'LL BE OK. WHAT DO YOU THINK?

WHATEVER YOU WEAR WILL BE LOVELY, DEAR.

Panel 4: ...THAT BAD, HUH?

Panel 5: WASN'T THERE ANYTHING HERE THAT YOU LIKED?

YES, BUT...

FERNANDO VASURA

ROMONA KEVEZA

Panel 6: JOHN AND I WANT TO MAKE YOUR WEDDING DRESS OUR GIFT TO YOU, DEANNA.

OH, ELLY!!!

Panel 7: I DON'T KNOW WHAT TO SAY! THIS HAS ALL BEEN SUCH A CRAZY EMOTIONAL MESS!

WEDDINGS ARE LIKE THAT, HONEY.

Panel 8: ...AND I STILL HAVE TWO KIDS LEFT TO GO.

Panel 9: ROMONA,—THIS IS THE DRESS I LIKE... MAY I TRY IT ON?

ABSOLUTELY.

Panel 10: AMAZING! IT FITS YOU SO WELL! MAYBE A SLIGHT ADJUSTMENT TO THE BACK... BUT THAT CAN BE DONE IN MINUTES!

Panel 11: IT'S STUNNING! I'D LOVE TO HAVE IT, ELLY- BUT, WHAT ABOUT MY MOTHER?

SHE SHOULD SEE IT, DEANNA. WE SHOULD CALL HER.

Panel 12: AFTER ALL THAT'S HAPPENED... WE DON'T WANT ANY MORE SURPRISES!

HELLO, MRS. SOBINSKI! HOW NICE TO SEE YOU AGAIN.

MY MOTHER'S HERE! SHE CAN'T SEE YOU, ELLY— NOT **NOW!**

I'M NOT SURE WHICH DRESSING ROOM DEANNA IS IN— LET ME CHECK FOR YOU.

YOU COME OUT, YOU HIDE— WE'LL WORK THIS OUT—TRUST ME!

I GUESS WHEN YOU'RE IN THE BRIDAL BUSINESS..., YOU LEARN HOW TO HANDLE ANYTHING!

THIS IS THE DRESS YOU ORDERED?

NO... I WAS JUST TRYING IT ON!

IT'S UNUSUAL.

I LOVE IT, MOM! AND DR. AND MRS. PATTERSON WANT TO HELP ME PAY FOR IT!

SO! THERE'S A CONSPIRACY GOING ON!!

WHAT **ELSE** ARE YOU HIDING FROM ME?

MRS. SOBINSKI, THIS IS A STRESSFUL TIME. PLEASE, SIT DOWN AND HAVE SOME TEA.— I WANT TO SHOW YOU SOMETHING.

THIS IS HOW YOUR BEAUTIFUL DAUGHTER WILL APPEAR ON HER WEDDING DAY.

OHHH

THE BOUQUET IS THE WRONG COLOR AND SHE NEEDS A NECKLACE, BUT... YOU REALLY DO LOOK LOVELY, DEAR!

THANKS, MOM!

Hi mom and Dad.
Camp is really fun. We are learning a lot about horses

We have to clean their stalls and brush them and then we get to ride. My horse is called Peppercorn.

We go canoeing and it is hard at first but I don't fall in now. At least not on purpose anyways.

Today we made kites. and a man who is Ojibway showed us some designs to draw and told us a history of his people.

We learned how to make pancakes and bannock and after that we had a relay swim which was so cool.

I have made lots of new friends and am learning lots of new things and I really really like it here a lot !!!!!!!!

except that I want to come HOME!

CAMPFIRE OUT? WE'VE HAD A GREAT DAY, EVERYONE. SADDLE UP. WE'RE HEADING OUT.

TROT.... TROT.... TROT.... TROT-TROT-TROT-TROT BUMP, BUMPITY, BUMP BUMP, BUMP

GALLOP, GALLOP GALLOP, GALLOP GALLOP....

AAAGHHHH

YES SIR, THESE TRIPS ALWAYS SEEM FASTER WHEN WE'RE COMING HOME!

SNORT

YEARS AGO, THE NATIVE PEOPLE CAMPED HERE. THIS IS WHERE SUMMER FOODS WERE GROWN AND GATHERED

IN WINTER, THE FAMILIES MOVED DOWN RIVER WHERE THEY WOULD HUNT AND TRAP.

WHERE WERE THEIR HOUSES?

THEY HAD PORTABLE ONES, MADE FROM SKINS-AND THEN, CANVASS. THEY ALSO MADE LODGES FROM LOGS AND MOSSES.

WHY DID THEY LEAVE?

THEY DIDN'T. THEIR SPIRITS ARE IN EVERY ANIMAL, EVERY ROCK AND EVERY TREE.

WHATCHA DOING, APRIL?

...LISTENING.

WELL, IT'S BEEN A GREAT TIME, PEOPLE! WE'VE HAD SOME ADVENTURES, LEARNED NEW SKILLS AND MADE NEW FRIENDS!

DID YOU CHECK YOUR CABINS FOR CLOTHES, DON'T FORGET YOUR CRAFTS AND COSTUMES

I KNOW SOME OF YOU WERE HOMESICK, BUT I HOPE THE LAST TWO WEEKS HAVE BEEN A LOT OF FUN FOR EVERYONE.

I'LL MISS YOU

CALL ME!

'BYE ALI'AH

SO LONG

'BYE APRIL

BYE JEFF

SEE YA!

CHART

BYE

SNIFF!

BYE

MMM - IT'S SO NICE TO HAVE YOU HOME FROM CAMP! - DID YOU HAVE FUN, HONEY?

YAH!

THERE WAS SIX KIDS TO A CABIN WITH BUNK BEDS! WE HAD ROW BOATS AN' CANOES AN' THE FOOD WAS AWESOME!

WE GOT DIVIDED INTO GROUPS SO WE ALL GOT TO RIDE THE HORSES AN' WE DID CRAFTS...

WHAT DID YOU LIKE MOST OF ALL?

-THERE WERE SOME REALLY, REALLY, REALLY HOT GUYS!!!

IT WAS SO COOL, MOM! THERE WERE 8 HORSES AN' WE ALL HAD TO LOOK AFTER THEM. IT WAS REALLY HARD WORK!

BUT WE WENT ON A TRAIL RIDE UP TO A BEAUTIFUL LAKE. IT WAS, LIKE OUT OF A MOVIE!

I HOPE YOU TOOK PICTURES!

UM..... I FORGOT.

TWO WEEKS AT CAMP AND YOU FORGOT TO TAKE ANY PICTURES?!!!!

DON'T WORRY, MOM - I'VE GOT LOTS OF THEM HERE IN MY HEAD!

HI, GRAMPA! LOOKIT ALL THE STUFF I BROUGHT HOME FROM CAMP!

WHAT'S THIS?

SWEET GRASS! MR. CROW WHO IS OJIBWA SHOWED US! YOU BRAID IT AND THEN YOU BURN IT FOR PRAYERS AND PURIFICATION.

- SNIFF?

YOU BRING THE SMOKE UP TO YOUR FACE LIKE THIS. YOU THANK MOTHER EARTH AND YOU REMEMBER YOUR ANCESTORS.

THAT'S A WONDER-FUL THING TO KNOW!

YAH! - AT FIRST I THOUGHT IT WAS SOMETHING YOU COULD EAT!

- CRUNCH?

MR. CROW TOLD US SOME LEGENDS AND STORIES ABOUT HIS PEOPLE. LATER SOME CHILDREN CAME AN' DANCED TO SINGING AND DRUMS.

THEY MADE BANNOCK WHICH IS A KIND OF BREAD COOKED OVER THE FIRE AND WE ATE IT WITH MAPLE SYRUP AN' BEANS!

MR. CROW SAYS ALL MEN ARE BROTHERS, AND IF YOU TAKE SOMETHING FROM THE EARTH, YOU MUST GIVE SOMETHING BACK. HE ALSO TOLD US TO LISTEN TO AND RESPECT OUR ELDERS

THAT'S A FINE PHILOSOPHY!

GRAMPA.... HOW COME INDIAN PEOPLE WERE CALLED "SAVAGES"?

WE MADE MASKS. THIS IS SUPPOSED TO BE A RAVEN, BUT I DIDN'T PAINT IT RIGHT.

GRAMPA, WHY DON'T WE HAVE TRADITIONAL DANCES AND COSTUMES LIKE THE FIRST NATIONS PEOPLE?

WE HAVE OUR TRADITIONS, APRIL.

BUT NOT LIKE OTHER KIDS! — DUTCH KIDS HAVE COSTUMES AN' SO DO GERMAN KIDS. IF YOU'RE FROM INDIA OR AFRICA OR JAPAN, THERE'S COSTUMES AN' SONGS AN' DANCES! EVEN ON THE EAST COAST AND IN QUEBEC, THEY HAVE TRADITIONAL CLOTHING AND DANCES AN' MUSIC!

WHAT DO WE DO HERE THAT MAKES US TRULY CANADIAN?

EH?

WHAT'S THIS?

GRAMPA'S MADE UP A TRADITIONAL CANADIAN COSTUME AN' A TRADITIONAL CANADIAN DANCE!

THIS SIGNIFIES THE LINE-UP AT TIM HORTON'S FOR COFFEE AND DOUGHNUTS

STOP SHUFFLE STOP SHUFFLE STOP

TAP, TAP TAP

THIS IS THE SWATTING OF FLIES WHILE TRYING TO START AN OUTBOARD MOTOR

AND THIS IS THE FROSTBITE FANDANGO... ALL TO THE ACCOMPANIMENT OF GUITAR, BUCKSAW AND SPOONS.

KNOCK KNOCK KNOCK

IF WE DON'T HAVE A GOOD SENSE OF OURSELVES... AT LEAST WE HAVE A GOOD SENSE OF HUMOR!

WAIT, WAIT, WAIT.....

OK! SNAP!

YOUR MOM'S DOG IS PRETTY SMART, ERIC!

YEAH!

WAIT FOR IT, NOW.... WAIT..... WAIT.... NOT YET.... WAIT....

OK!! SNAPP!

GOOD BOY! SAMMY IS SUCH A GOOOOD BOY!!!!

THAT DOESN'T LOOK LIKE SUCH A HARD TRICK TO DO!

CHEESE CUBES

BEE SNAX

SNAP!

CANDACE! WHERE ARE YOU GUYS GOING?

TO THE DOCTOR. RUDY HURT HIS NECK!

AND HE WON'T LET ME TELL YOU HOW!!

LYNN

SHE'S RUNNING OK NOW, DOC – BUT THIS IS GETTING TO BE AN OLD CAR!

I KNOW.

I'VE BEEN LOOKING AROUND, BUT WITH ELIZABETH STILL IN SCHOOL, AND MICHAEL GETTING MARRIED....

I HAVE SOMETHING TO SHOW YOU.

A 1962 BUSHWHACKER 4X! FRAME OFF RESTORATION, REBUILT ENGINE, BLUE-PRINTED AND BALANCED, MAG WHEELS, CLEAR COATED, CANDY APPLE RED!!

....DOES THIS MEAN YOU'RE INTERESTED?

A BUSHWHACKER 4X CONVERTIBLE! GORD, EVER SINCE I WAS A KID, I'VE WANTED ONE OF THESE!

BUT, WHAT I NEED IS A NEW CAR!

THIS IS A NEW CAR! LIKE I SAID, COMPLETELY REBUILT– THIS BABY IS A CLASSIC!!

THESE CARS ARE SO IMPRACTICAL. THEY'RE ROUGH RIDING, COLD IN WINTER ... ELLY WOULD THINK I WAS CRAZY IF I BOUGHT ONE, SO DON'T EVEN TEMPT ME!

I'LL TAKE A TRADE IN.

WHERE ARE THE KEYS?

GARAGE

TAKE 'ER FOR A SPIN, JOHN. JUST SEE IF SHE ISN'T THE SWEETEST LITTLE DEAL IN THE CITY!

YEAH, THIS IS THE LIFE! I FEEL LIKE I'M 20 AGAIN!

BEEP BEEP!

... I JUST WISHED I **LOOKED** LIKE I WAS 20 AGAIN!

VROOM!

HONEY, COULD YOU COME OUTSIDE? I WANT YOU TO SEE SOMETHING!

A COMPLETELY REBUILT 1962 BUSH-WHACKER 4X CONVERTIBLE! I'VE WANTED ONE OF THESE SINCE I WAS A KID! - IT WAS AT GORD'S GARAGE! .... WHAT DO YOU THINK?

WELL?!!

I THINK YOU'RE NUTS.

BUT, I HAVEN'T DECIDED TO BUY IT YET.

...YOU WILL.

WHAT WAS THAT ALL ABOUT?

JOHN WANTS TO TRADE HIS CAR IN ON A 1962 BUSHWHACKER CONVERTIBLE.

I TOLD HIM HE WAS CRAZY, BUT TO GO AHEAD AND BUY IT ANYWAY. AFTER ALL, IT'LL BE A GOOD INVESTMENT.

A CAR ISN'T A GOOD INVESTMENT, EL!

NO....

BUT THE MARRIAGE IS!

YOU BOUGHT THE CAR!

NOT YET. GORD LET ME BORROW IT FOR A WEEK - JUST TO MAKE SURE.

WHOA! CHECK IT OUT! CAN WE GO FOR A DRIVE, DAD?

COMING?

THIS IS SOOO COOL!!!

YES SIR, THE FOLKS WHO DRIVE THESE CARS ARE DIFFERENT! THEY'RE A BREED APART!

RIGHT!

...THEY ALL LOOK LIKE THIS!

MOM, WHY DO THEY CALL THESE "POT LUCK" DINNERS?

...I DON'T SEE ANY POTS!

HEY, LIZ! GUESS WHAT! DAD WIERDED OUT AND TRADED HIS CAR IN ON A 1962 BUSHWHACKER CONVERTIBLE!

IT'S CANDY APPLE RED WITH A BLACK ROOF THAT COMES OFF AND SO DO THE DOORS! IT'S GOT A ROLL BAR, AND YOU CAN FOLD DOWN THE BACK SEATS AND FILL IT FULL OF JUNK!

MOM SAYS HE'S TRYING TO RELIVE HIS CHILDHOOD BY BUYING THE CAR HE ALWAYS WANTED TO HAVE WHEN HE WAS A KID!

THAT MEANS, WHEN I'M 50, I'LL BE TRYING TO FIND A CAR THAT'S EXACTLY THE SAME AS THE ONE DAD JUST SOLD!

WHAT'S UP, LIZ?

I'M STUNNED! MY DAD JUST SOLD HIS SPORTSCAR. HE'S HAD IT FOR AGES!

MAN, SO MUCH IS HAPPENING AND I FEEL TOTALLY LEFT OUT. — I CAN'T WAIT TO GO HOME FOR THE WEDDING!

YOU'RE COMING WITH ME, AREN'T YOU?

I DUNNO... I GET SO EMOTIONAL, IT'S EMBAR-RASSING!

YOU CRY AT WEDDINGS, ERIC?

YEAH.

I ALWAYS FEEL SO SORRY FOR THE GUY!!

LIZ JUST E-MAILED ME BACK, MOM. SHE SAYS HER BRIDE'S MAID'S DRESS FITS FINE, BUT IT NEEDS TO BE TAKEN IN UNDER THE ARMS.

SHE SAYS SHE STILL ISN'T SURE IF ERIC WILL COME TO THE WEDDING.... BUT SHE HOPES HE WILL.

SHE SAYS SHE REALLY MISSES EVERYONE AND TO GIVE EDDY A GREAT BIG HUG FROM HER.

.... YOU FIRST!

SLUPP SLUPP SLORPP

95

HERE SHE IS, TED! MY NEW BABY!

NOT BAD, JOHN. A REAL CLASSIC CAR! IN GREAT SHAPE, TOO.

I'M SURPRISED ELLY LET YOU BUY IT!

ARE YOU KIDDING? THIS WAS ENTIRELY MY DECISION!

THANK YOU, THANK YOU, THANK YOU, THANK YOU!

JOHN CERTAINLY LOVES HIS NEW CAR, EL.

I KNOW. HE'S SO HAPPY.

YOU KNOW, CONNIE..... THERE'S NOTHING IN THIS WORLD THAT I JUST HAVE TO HAVE!

THERE ISN'T A CAR OR A COAT OR AN APPLIANCE .... I DON'T WANT CLOTHES OR FURNITURE—THERE'S NOTHING I REALLY WANT OR NEED!

HOW ABOUT GRAND CHILDREN?

..."THEY'RE SOMETHING I "LONG FOR."

WHERE'S YOUR DAD GOING?

OUT, WITH HIS FRIEND, IRIS

ISN'T IT NICE THAT PEOPLE THEIR AGE CAN HAVE A LOVE AFFAIR?

I THINK IT'S NICE AT ANY AGE!

DO YOU THINK THEY'LL GET MARRIED?

CONNIE, WITH MIKE AND DEE'S WEDDING COMING UP.... I DON'T WANT TO THINK ABOUT IT.

COME ON, EL! WHAT'S SO HARD ABOUT BEING MOTHER OF THE GROOM?

...STAYING FRIENDS WITH THE MOTHER OF THE BRIDE!

HELLO, ELLY? IT'S MIRA! HOW ARE YOU?—THAT'S FINE....

I'M JUST CALLING TO TELL YOU THAT I'M CHANGING MY "MOTHER OF THE BRIDE" ENSEMBLE FROM NAVY TO VIOLET

THAT'S WHAT I'M WEARING!

I THOUGHT WE MIGHT LOOK TOO SIMILAR, SO I HOPE YOU CAN FIND SOMETHING IN ANOTHER COLOR.

BUT, MIRA...

I BOUGHT MY SUIT AGES AGO!—WHEN THE KIDS FIRST MADE THEIR ANNOUNCEMENT!

THEN I'M DOING YOU A FAVOR DEAR!

IT'S PROBABLY OUT OF STYLE!

WHO WAS THAT?

MIRA SOBINSKI. SHE WANTS ME TO FIND A DIFFERENT COLORED OUTFIT TO WEAR TO THE WEDDING.

YOU'VE GOT LOTS OF CLOTHES, HONEY!

THAT'S NOT THE POINT! I'VE HAD MY SUIT FOR MONTHS NOW. IT'S NOT FAIR!!!

WELL, THIS GIVES YOU A CHANCE TO GO SHOPPING!

I DON'T **WANT** TO GO SHOPPING!!

A WOMAN CANNOT SHOP FOR CLOTHING IF SHE FEELS OVER WEIGHT OR ANGRY!

HEY, WEED, HOW'S IT GOIN'?

FINE. I'VE GOT ALL THE PIX FOR THE BRONSON ACCOUNT!

WHERE'S THE LITTLE WOMAN?

THE GIRLS AT WORK TOOK HER OUT FOR DINNER. THEY'RE GIVING HER A WEDDING SHOWER!

TOO BAD THERE ISN'T A DEAL LIKE THAT FOR THE GUYS. YOU COULD GET JUMPER CABLE GIFT SETS HIS & HERS FLASHLIGHTS A DELUXE WEED WHACKER, BEER COOLER, STAPLE GUN, OR MONO-GRAMMED UNDER SHORTS....

INSTEAD, WE JUST TAKE YOU OUT FOR ONE LAST NIGHT ON THE TOWN, AND GET YOU HOPELESSLY RIPPED!

WHAT?!!

99

APRIL, YOUR DRESS IS HERE!

FOR THE WEDDING? LEMME SEE!!!

IT'S PALE BLUE WITH WHITE AND YELLOW FLOWERS!

IT'S GOING TO MATCH THE RING BEARER'S SUIT, WHICH WILL BE PALE BLUE WITH A WHITE SHIRT AND YELLOW BOW TIE!

RING BEARER?

YES. DEANNA'S LITTLE NEPHEW, SEAN, WILL BE CARRYING THE RINGS.

THEN WHAT WILL I DO?

YOU'LL BE CARRYING A BASKET OF FLOWERS

IS THAT ALL?

NO. YOU AND SEAN GET TO GO DOWN THE AISLE FIRST, FOLLOWED BY THE BRIDES-MAIDS AND THEN THE BRIDE!

BUT, WHAT DO I ACTUALLY DO?!!

BE ON YOUR BEST BEHAVIOUR OR ELSE!

OH

.....I KNEW IT WOULD BE SOMETHING DIFFICULT!!

LYNN

ELIZABETH! IT'S SO GOOD TO SEE YOU!

I SURE MISSED YOU!

WHERE'S ERIC?

HE COULDN'T COME, SO I TOOK THE BUS!

I THOUGHT THIS YOUNG MAN OF YOURS WOULD AT LEAST ESCORT YOU TO YOUR BROTHER'S WEDDING!

MOM... IT'S NO BIG DEAL.

WE DON'T OWN EACH OTHER!

NO...BUT SOMETIMES YOU "OWE" EACH OTHER!

MMM-IT'S SO GOOD TO BE HOME!

WE DON'T HAVE MUCH TIME, HONEY.

I WANT YOU BOTH TO TRY YOUR DRESSES ON.

AWW GEE ... I'VE TRIED IT ON A LOT OF TIMES ALREADY!

WELL, THERE'S ONE GOOD THING - AT LEAST THEY DON'T LOOK LIKE BRIDESMAID AND FLOWER GIRL DRESSES!

WHAT DO YOU MEAN?

WE'LL BE ABLE TO WEAR THEM AGAIN!

GUESS WHAT, LIZ! WE GET TO HAVE OUR HAIR DONE UP WITH LITTLE WHITE FLOWERS.

OH, YEAH?

MRS. SOBINSKI SENT US A PICTURE OF HOW WE SHOULD LOOK.

SAUSAGE CURLS? EWWW! NOBODY WEARS SAUSAGE CURLS!!

MOM, THIS IS SO 60's !!!!

DON'T FUSS ABOUT YOUR HAIR. THE STYLIST WILL PUT IT UP, AND YOU'LL LOOK JUST FINE.

HOW ARE YOU GONNA WEAR YOUR HAIR?

... I WAS GOING TO HAVE IT DONE IN SAUSAGE CURLS.

I DON'T KNOW WHAT IT IS, ELLY... BUT, SOMETHING'S WRONG WITH THE WAY WE'VE DECORATED THE PEWS.

WE HAVE ALL THE BOWS TIED, MRS. SOBINSKI - AND THE FLOWERS WILL BE HERE ANY MINUTE.

THANK YOU, TRACEY

MICHAEL, MAY I HAVE A WORD WITH YOU?

SURE THING!

WHY DIDN'T YOU HAVE GORDON BE YOUR BEST MAN? I FIND YOUR CHOICE OF LAWRENCE RATHER ODD

OH?

BUT MIRA - WE'VE KNOWN EACH OTHER SINCE WE WERE KIDS!

I'VE JUST BEEN TOLD THAT HE IS A HOMO-SEXUAL!

REALLY?

... I JUST THOUGHT HE WAS GAY!

I'M NOT COMFORTABLE HAVING LAWRENCE IN THE WEDDING PARTY, MICHAEL.

WELL... MAYBE YOU SHOULD TELL HIM!

LAWRENCE? - DEANNA'S MOM WANTS TO TALK TO YOU!

SURE! HI, MRS. SOBINSKI! HOW CAN I HELP YOU?

WELL ... TO BEGIN WITH .... I DID NOT KNOW YOU WERE, UM.....

GAY?!!

WELL, DON'T WORRY. I NEVER DRESS IN DRAG!

BUT IF I DID, TRUST ME - I WOULD DO NOTHING TO OUTSHINE THE BRIDE !!!

102

MOTHER, HOW DARE YOU TELL MICHAEL WHO HE SHOULD CHOOSE TO BE THE BEST MAN?!!

I DON'T WANT A GAY PERSON IN THE WEDDING PARTY!

LAWRENCE IS A DECENT MAN!

HE'S HONEST AND CARING AND WELL EDUCATED! HE'S A LAW ABIDING, PRODUCTIVE CITIZEN.

BESIDES THAT, HE'S A WONDERFUL FRIEND AND A FINE HUMAN BEING.

BUT DEANNA...

THIS IS A CHURCH !!!

MOTHER, I AM SICK AND TIRED OF YOU TRYING TO RUN OUR LIVES!!

YOU CHOSE THE COLORS, THE FLOWERS, THE MUSIC THE FOOD! YOU DECIDED ON THE CLOTHING, THE SERVICE AND THE RECEPTION! ...

AND NOW, JUST BEFORE THE CEREMONY— YOU'RE TELLING US WHO WE CAN AND CANNOT HAVE IN THE WEDDING PARTY!

AAWHHH!

YOU NEVER APPRECIATE ANYTHING I DO FOR YOU!!!!

MOM, WHAT'S GOING ON?

IT'S THE "LAST MINUTE MELT-DOWN," APRIL.

JUST BEFORE A WEDDING, SOMETHING USUALLY GOES WRONG. TEARS FLOW, TEMPERS FLARE –AND PEOPLE OFTEN SAY THINGS THEY WISH THEY HADN'T SAID.

IT'S ALL PART OF THE DAY. IT'S ONE OF THE THINGS THAT MAKES A WEDDING MAGICAL.

MAGICAL?

UH HUH...BECAUSE, DESPITE ALL OF THE TENSION AND TANTRUMS-THINGS ALWAYS TURN OUT BEAUTIFULLY.

Panel 1: THAT WAS A BEAUTIFUL WEDDING, MIRA. YOU DID AN OUTSTANDING JOB!
I DID MY BEST, JOHN.

Panel 2: I WOULD HAVE MADE EVERYTHING MORE ELEGANT, BUT WILF AND MICHAEL WOULDN'T LET ME.

Panel 3: SO, WE'RE HAVING THE RECEPTION AT THE CLUB — AND I'VE TRIED TO BE MOST REASONABLE WITH MY REQUESTS.

Panel 4: — IT'S JUST UNFORTUNATE THEY WEREN'T ABLE TO REPAINT THE EXTERIOR !!

HIGHCREST
OLF & COUNTRY

Panel 5: MOM, DO SEAN AND I HAVE TO SIT AT THE HEAD TABLE?
NO, HONEY. YOU CAN SIT WITH US.

Panel 6: WHY DO THEY CALL THAT A "HEAD TABLE"?
'CAUSE THEY GET TO EAT AHEAD OF EVERYONE ELSE.

Panel 7: WHAT ARE THESE?
CORNISH GAME HENS.
WHAT KIND OF GAME DO THEY PLAY?
I DUNNO.

Panel 8: ...BUT, IT LOOKS LIKE THEY LOST!

Panel 9: WHAT'S HAPPENING NOW?
LAWRENCE HAS TO MAKE A TOAST TO MICHAEL AN' DEANNA.

Panel 10: MICHAEL, I HAVE KNOWN YOU SINCE WE WERE CHILDREN. YOU ARE ONE OF MY CLOSEST AND MOST TRUSTED FRIENDS.

Panel 11: I ALWAYS WONDERED WHERE YOUR MANY TALENTS WOULD LEAD YOU, AND WHO WOULD SHARE YOUR JOURNEY ALONG THE WAY.

Panel 12: DO TOASTS TAKE A LONG TIME, APRIL?
I THINK IT DEPENDS ON THE TOASTER.

DEANNA, YOU ARE KIND AND GRACIOUS, INTELLIGENT AND LOVING. YOUR WARMTH AND YOUR HUMOR SHINE THROUGH YOUR SMILE.

I BELIEVE IT WAS MORE THAN LUCK OR COIN-CIDENCE THAT BROUGHT YOU TWO TOGETHER. I BELIEVE THAT SOME THINGS ARE "MEANT TO BE".

MAY YOUR LIVES ALWAYS BE RICH WITH LOVE AND ADVENTURE. MAY YOU LIVE IN HEALTH AND HARMONY — AND, MAY WE CELEBRATE FOR MANY YEARS TO COME — THIS DAY, THESE VOWS... THIS UNION.

LADIES AND GENTLEMEN.. ...TO THE GRIDE AND BROOM!!

As they drove away in his father's car, Michael put his arm around Deanna. She was wearing his jacket and holding down the front of the now billowing wedding dress. The ceremony her mother had orchestrated in such detail was over. It hadn't been an ordeal—it had been a celebration.

Married, before friends and family, they went home to do what couples do: the dishes, the laundry, and the bills.

JOHN, I KNOW YOU LOVE YOUR NEW CAR, BUT ISN'T IT TIME TO PUT THE TOP AND THE DOORS ON?

THANKS FOR MEETING ME, ERIC.

HEY, NO PROBLEM! HOW WAS THE WEDDING?

BEAUTIFUL, ACTUALLY. SO MANY PEOPLE WERE THERE! MY DAD'S PARENTS, MY COUSINS, FRIENDS—THEY ALL WANTED TO MEET YOU!

YEAH?

...TOO BAD IT DIDN'T WORK OUT.

DID YOU MISS ME?

THAT'S A DUMB QUESTION!

I KNOW... BUT, DID YOU MISS ME?

Lynn

WHOA! WHAT HAPPENED?

GUESS WE GOT A LITTLE BEHIND IN THE HOUSEKEEPING DEPARTMENT!

PORK PUFFS

THIS PLACE IS A MESS! I HOPE YOU DON'T EXPECT ME TO CLEAN IT UP!

NO WAY!

JUST IGNORE EVERYTHING, LIZ.—WE'LL GET AROUND TO IT SOMETIME!

Lynn

MEN! JUST LOOK AT THIS PLACE! HOW CAN THEY **FIND** ANYTHING?!!

TACO BOMBS

WHAT'S THIS?

THIS IS NOT ONE OF MY HAIR CLIPS—AND THIS ISN'T MY HAIR!

ERIC, DID YOU HAVE ANOTHER GIRL IN THE APARTMENT WHILE I WAS AWAY?

WHAT KIND OF A QUESTION IS THAT?

I HOPE IT'S ONE THAT WILL GET AN HONEST ANSWER!

ERIC, WERE YOU SEEING SOMEONE ELSE WHILE I WAS AT MY BROTHER'S WEDDING?

LIZ, I CAN'T BELIEVE YOU'RE ASKING ME THAT!

WHO'S HAIR CLIP IS THIS?

HEY, I DUNNO! I THOUGHT IT WAS YOURS! —WHAT'S THE MATTER? DON'T YOU TRUST ME?!

'CAUSE IF YOU DON'T TRUST ME, WE MIGHT AS WELL END THIS RELATIONSHIP RIGHT NOW.

OF COURSE I TRUST YOU!

GOOD. THEN THAT ANSWERS YOUR QUESTION. DOESN'T IT.

HAVE YOU HEARD FROM ELIZABETH, DEAR?

YES, DAD. SHE GOT HOME SAFELY, SCHOOL IS HECTIC, BUT, SHE'S PLEASED WITH HER COURSES AND IS GLAD TO BE BACK UP NORTH.

SHE SOUNDED OK, BUT, I COULDN'T HELP THINKING THERE WAS SOMETHING SHE WASN'T TELLING ME.

THERE ARE ALWAYS THINGS KIDS DON'T TELL THEIR PARENTS, ELLY. I'M SURE YOU HAVEN'T TOLD ME EVERYTHING!

YOU'RE RIGHT, DAD... I HAVEN'T.

—AND, I'M NOT GOING TO START TELLING YOU NOW!

SNIFFF!

I LOVE AUTUMN. I LOVE THE COLORS AND THE SMELL AND THE FEEL OF AUTUMN!

BWAAAAAAAAAAAHHH

I JUST CAN'T GET USED TO THE SOUND OF IT!!

WHAT?!!

HONEY, COULD YOU HELP ME GET RID OF THESE LEAVES, PLEASE?

AWW, DAD!

GO AND GET THE BAGS FROM THE GARAGE.

TSK. CAN'T I DO IT LATER?!!

NO, I WANT IT DONE NOW!

BUT, I'M S'POSED TO MEET SOME OF MY FRIENDS!

JUST GO GET THE BAGS, OK?!

OK!

OH, FOR HEAVEN'S SAKE, APRIL!!!

XTRA LARGE GARDEN BAGS

GUESS WHAT, MOM! DAD JUST TOLD ME TO STOP ACTING LIKE A TEEN-AGER!

LOOK, JOHN. I BROUGHT HOME A BOOK FOR APRIL THAT EXPLAINS MATURITY AND EVERYTHING ABOUT HUMAN REPRODUCTION.

THESE ARE ALL THE THINGS SHE'S UNCOMFORTABLE TALKING ABOUT!

I'M GOING TO PUT IT RIGHT HERE IN THE BOOK SHELF AND I'M NOT GOING TO SAY A THING. WHEN IT'S MOVED—I'LL KNOW SHE'S BEEN READING IT.

GUESS WHAT! WE HAFTA DO A PROJECT ON CONIFEROUS TREES.

I THINK WE HAVE SOME GOOD NATURE BOOKS—YOU SHOULD CHECK THE BOOK SHELF!

BIRDS OF EASTERN CANADA, EDIBLE MUSHROOMS, THE ART OF ROBERT BATEMAN.... —WHAT'S THIS?!!

WOW. I DIDN'T KNOW WE HAD A BOOK ABOUT SEX!—AN' IT LOOKS BRAND NEW!

THERE MUST BE SOMETHING IN HERE THAT MOM DIDN'T KNOW!

BECKY, YOU WON'T BELIEVE THIS, BUT I FOUND A BOOK AT HOME THAT EXPLAINS EVERYTHING ABOUT ... YOU KNOW...EVERYTHING!

YEAH! ALL THAT STUFF! ...LIKE PUBERTY AN' HOW YOUR BODY CHANGES. IT EVEN HAS COOL ILLUSTRATIONS!

NO! OF COURSE I CAN'T BRING IT OVER TO YOUR HOUSE!

I'M PROBABLY NOT EVEN SUPPOSED TO BE READING IT!!

117

LOOK, JOHN. I PUT "THE BOOK" BETWEEN DISCOVERING ANIMALS AND THE MacMILLAN VISUAL DICTIONARY.

IT'S NOW BETWEEN "ART OF THE INCAS" AND "THE WORLD ATLAS!"

SO, SHE'S READING IT!

APRIL'S LEARNING ABOUT REPRODUCTION FROM A PROFESSIONAL WHO EXPLAINS EVERYTHING SO KIDS CAN UNDERSTAND!

I LEARNED EVERYTHING FROM ROCKY FIGGWORT WHO HEARD IT FROM STAN GELDING, WHO HEARD IT FROM HIS OLDER BROTHER BERT....

WHO SAID HE'D "DONE IT."

IN THOSE DAYS, WE LEARNED BY WORD OF MYTH.

THIS IS A MAJORLY COOL BOOK!

CHECK OUT THIS PAGE BECKY!

DID YOUR MOM JUST GIVE IT TO YOU?

NO WAY! I FOUND IT IN THE BOOK SHELF.

THE BIG ? QUESTION

THE BOOKSHELF? LIKE, IT SUDDENLY APPEARED? HEY, YOUR MOM SELLS BOOKS, MAN! THIS IS A "PLANT", APRIL — SHE WANTED YOU TO READ IT!

REALLY ?

HOO! I CAN'T BELIEVE I DID SOMETHING MY MOM ACTUALLY WANTED ME TO DO!!

IS THIS YOUR PROJECT ON CONIFEROUS TREES, HONEY?

COULD I SEE IT?

UH-HUH. SURE

BUT, DIDN'T YOU READ IT ALREADY?

WELL... I MIGHT HAVE TAKEN A QUICK LOOK WHEN I BROUGHT UP THE LAUNDRY.

....HOW DID YOU KNOW?

YOU MOVED IT FROM THE HEART TO THE FLOWER!

BUT, THAT'S OK, MOM. I KNOW WHEN YOU DO STUFF ....IT'S FROM THE HEART.

I HAVE A DECIDUOUS FAMILY... EVERY FALL, THEY START SHEDDING.

YOU TOOK SOME GREAT PHOTOGRAPHS OF THE WEDDING, JO.

YEAH. THEY TURNED OUT OK!

I PUT ALBUMS TOGETHER FOR THE FOLKS, ONE FOR US AND ONE FOR YOU.

EXCELLENT!

THE ONLY PROBLEM I HAD WAS WITH THE ENLARGEMENTS I DID FOR DEE'S MOTHER.

WHAT WAS WRONG WITH THEM?

SHE SAID THEY MADE HER LOOK "BIGGER".

JUST OUT OF CURIOSITY, ...WHAT DID YOU DO WITH YOUR DRESS?

I HAD IT BOXED FOR STORAGE

WOW. I WONDER HOW MANY WEDDING DRESSES ARE STORED IN CLOSETS AND ATTICS.—WE SHOULD DO A STORY ON THIS MIKE!

I'LL CALL THE MAGAZINE AN' SUGGEST A SPRING FOCUS SECTION ON THINGS CELEBRITIES HAVE SAVED FROM THEIR WEDDINGS!!

THEY SAVE CARDS AND LETTERS, BOUQUETS AND PIECES OF CAKE! ...WHERE SHOULD WE BEGIN?

PROBABLY WITH THE ONES WHO'VE SAVED THEIR MARRIAGES!

WHAT'S ALL THIS?

APARTMENTS FOR RENT.

WE HAVE TO MOVE, WEED.

THE GUY WHO OWNS THIS HOUSE IS COMING BACK AT THE END OF THE MONTH

THAT'S LESS THAN 2 WEEKS! WHAT ARE YOU DOING?!

WE'VE BEEN LOOKING—WE JUST CAN'T AFFORD WHAT'S OUT THERE.

THERE ARE NO APARTMENTS IN OUR PRICE RANGE!

HOME, HOME IN THE RAAANGE....

THAT'S NOT FUNNY. —

WE'RE SO LUCKY TO HAVE HAD THIS PLACE. WE'VE BEEN HOUSE-SITTING AND LOOKING AFTER LAWRENCE'S FRIEND'S PLANTS...

SO, THE RENT'S BEEN VERY LOW —NOW, WE HAVE TO CHECK OUT THE REAL WORLD!

THERE'S A NICE LITTLE APARTMENT COMING UP NEXT TO ME, IF YOU'RE INTERESTED.

REALLY? I HAVEN'T SEEN IT ADVERTISED

THE LADY WHO OWNS THE HOUSE FINDS TENANTS PRIVATELY. SHE SAYS SHE LIKES TO MEET THEM, FACE TO FACE.

I LIKE THIS NEIGHBORHOOD, JO.

IT SUITS ME!

MRS. SALTZMAN, THIS IS MIKE AN' DEANNA PATTERSON.

TO SEE THE APARTMENT, RIGHT?

IF YOU DON'T MIND.

MIND? WHY SHOULD I MIND!—AN EMPTY APARTMENT DOES ME NO GOOD!

IF I DON'T SHOW IT, YOU DON'T SEE IT. IF YOU DON'T SEE IT, YOU DON'T TAKE IT. IF YOU DON'T TAKE IT, I HAVE AN EMPTY APARTMENT.

SO, ... YOU'LL SEE IT.

IT'S NARROW, BUT COMFY, YOU GOT EVERYTHING... KITCHEN, BEDROOM AND A FULL BATH.

THE KITCHEN NEEDS REPAIRS. I WISH I COULD FIND SOMEONE TO FIX THIS PLACE UP.

MY HUSBAND, WITH HIS BACK—CAN HARDLY PICK UP THE NEWSPAPER.

MRS. SALTZMAN?

I CAN'T GET THE TUB TO DRAIN.

LIKE I SAID... IT COMES WITH A FULL BATH.

IT'S GETTING COLDER, JIM. I CAN SMELL THE FROST IN THE AIR!

WINTER'S COMING. I CAN FEEL IT IN MY BONES!

I CAN FEEL IT EVERYWHERE!

I GUESS YOU COULD SAY WE'RE IN THE WINTER OF OUR LIVES!

I'M NOT SURE I LIKE THAT EXPRESSION!

I DO!

IN THE "SPRING OF YOUR LIFE", YOU'RE SILLY AND OUT OF CONTROL. — IN THE "SUMMER", YOU'RE HAVING BABIES, PAYING MORTGAGES AND STRUGGLING WITH CAREERS...

IN THE "AUTUMN OF YOUR LIFE", YOU HAVE CHILDREN TO PUT THROUGH UNIVERSITY .... AND THE SHOCK OF DISCOVERING YOU'RE NOT GETTING ANY YOUNGER...

BUT WINTER CAN BE THE BEST TIME OF ALL!

WHY?!

...WE CAN JUST LOOK FORWARD TO A LONG, WARM, HAPPY ONE!

SO, YOU'VE SEEN THE APARTMENT. IT'S AVAILABLE NOW. I'LL LEAVE YOU IN PRIVATE TO TALK IT OVER.

THANKS, MRS. SALTZMAN.

WELL?

IT'S NICE, BUT IT NEEDS A LOT OF WORK, WEED!

AND, IT'S EXPENSIVE.

DO YOU THINK SHE WOULD LOWER THE RENT A LITTLE IF WE DID ALL THE REPAIRS?

THAT COULD BE ARRANGED.

YES! WE WOULD LIKE TO TAKE THE APARTMENT!

GOOD. YOU LOOK LIKE A NICE COUPLE.

WE'LL DRAW UP AN AGREEMENT REGARDING THE REPAIRS, AND I'LL NEED YOUR FIRST AND LAST MONTHS' RENT.

I ALSO NEED REFERENCES.

HERE'S A LIST OF NAMES AND ADDRESSES... AND I'LL CALL MY FOLKS.

MIKE, CAN PARENTS GIVE YOU A REFERENCE?

I DUNNO... I'M HOPING THEY'LL GIVE US THE RENT!

FIRST AND LAST MONTHS' RENT? MIKE, THAT'S OVER 2000 BUCKS!!

SORRY, DAD - I HATE TO ASK.

BUT, THE PLACE WE'RE MOVING TO IS UNFURNISHED. THERE'S A LOAD OF STUFF WE HAVE TO BUY, AND...

YOU WILL?!! WOW, THANKS! - AND DON'T WORRY, WE'LL PAY IT ALL BACK - WITH INTEREST!

IT'S SO NICE TO HAVE PARENTS YOU CAN BANK ON!

ELLY, YOUR WINDOW DISPLAYS ARE FANTASTIC!

THANKS, ANNE!

I'VE BEEN TAKING A DIFFERENT ROUTE TO WORK, JUST SO I CAN SEE THE DOWNTOWN DECORATIONS!

I THOUGHT I'D IGNORE HALLOWE'EN AFTER THE KIDS GREW UP - BUT THE OLDER I GET, THE MORE I ENJOY IT.

ME TOO

I'VE STARTED TO RELATE TO THE PUMPKINS.

IS JOHN GOING TO DECORATE HIS GARDEN RAILWAY AGAIN?

HE'S ALREADY STARTED.

THIS YEAR, HE PUT IN A HAUNTED HOUSE - AND EVEN RENTED A FULL-SIZED PLASTIC WITCH.

REALLY!

WHY ON EARTH WOULD HE DO THAT?

...IT'S A ROLE I DECIDED TO TURN DOWN.

SNUFFAH WHUFF SNIFF SNERF...

?

BARK BARK YONF YARP YAP YAP YAP!

YIIIPE!!

HI DEANNA! HI, MICHAEL—LOOK WHAT DADDY AN' I DID!

AMAZING!

WE PUT COBWEBS ON THE MODEL TRAIN STATION, AN' BUILT A HAUNTED HOUSE!

I BET EVERYONE'S GONNA COME AN' SEE HIS HALLOWE'EN DISPLAY THIS YEAR!

YEAH!

LOOKS LIKE YOUR MOTHER'S ALREADY HERE!

WHAP!

HOW COME YOU GUYS ARE HERE?

MOM SAID WE COULD HAVE THE RECROOM FURNITURE.

BUT THAT'S WHERE I LIVE!

SHE'S GONNA GET NEW STUFF, APRIL!

I DON'T WANT NEW STUFF. I LIKE THAT COUCH. I EAT POPCORN AN' PIZZA AN' WATCH TV ON THAT COUCH!

YOU CAN DO ALL THOSE THINGS ON A NEW ONE!

BUT WHERE WOULD I WIPE MY HANDS?

ELLY, YOU GAVE MIKE AND DEANNA ALL THE RECROOM FURNITURE?

WE TALKED ABOUT IT, JOHN!

THE COFFEE TABLE? THE LAMPS? THE TELEVISION?

THEY NEED THEM MORE THAN WE DO, HONEY.

OH.

MAN, WHEN THESE GUYS GIVE STUFF AWAY ON HALLOWE'EN, THEY REALLY GIVE STUFF AWAY!

TRICK OR TREAT

TRICK OR TREAT

THAT WAS A NICE HALLOWE'EN, EL. WE HAD A LOT OF KIDS THIS YEAR!

WE'RE GOING TO BRING IN YOUR DISPLAY, DAD.

THANKS—I DON'T WANT TO LEAVE ANYTHING OUT!

WHAT WOULD YOU LIKE US TO DO WITH THE WITCH?

I HAVE TO TAKE HER BACK TO THE RENTAL SHOP TOMORROW, SO YOU CAN PUT HER IN MY CAR.

...TRY THE PASSENGER SIDE !!!

DARN, I'M LATE FOR WORK! GOTTA RUN, HONEY—HAVE A GOOD DAY.

IF I'M LUCKY, THE RENTAL SHOP WILL BE OPEN, AND I CAN DROP YOU OFF ON MY WAY TO THE CLINIC.

NEXT TIME I TAKE YOU OUT, ...BRUSH YOUR TEETH AND USE A LITTLE MOISTURIZER!

RATS. THIS PLACE DOESN'T OPEN UNTIL 10!

JOE & MILDRED'S
JOKES · SMOKES · NOVELTIES

COSTUME RENTALS

I DON'T WANT TO LEAVE YOU IN THE CAR, SO I'D BETTER TAKE YOU UP TO THE CLINIC.

DR. PATTERSON... WHY IS A WITCH SITTING IN THE WAITING ROOM?

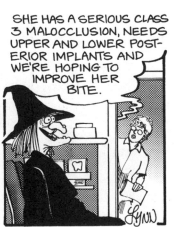

SHE HAS A SERIOUS CLASS 3 MALOCCLUSION, NEEDS UPPER AND LOWER POSTERIOR IMPLANTS AND WE'RE HOPING TO IMPROVE HER BITE.

ELLY, I CAN'T BELIEVE YOU GAVE MIKE AND DEANNA ALL OUR REC ROOM FURNITURE!

I'M SORRY, JOHN....WE TALKED ABOUT GETTING NEW THINGS!

THAT WAS BEFORE THEY BORROWED MONEY FOR THEIR RENT! WE'RE ALSO HELPING TO SUPPORT ELIZABETH—AND THE STORE JUST BARELY TURNED A PROFIT THIS QUARTER.

RIGHT.

WE SHOULD HAVE LET THEM FIND SECOND HAND STUFF IN THE PAPER.—THERE'S ALWAYS GREAT STUFF IN THE PAPER!

WHATCHA DOING, MOM?

....LOOKING FOR FURNITURE.

DON'T TELL ME YOU BOUGHT THAT COUCH SECOND HAND!

AND THE COFFEE TABLE!

HARDLY A SCRATCH ON IT!—ACTUALLY, IT'S BETTER THAN THE ONE WE HAD!

I GOT THE WALL UNIT AT "SECOND HAND ROSE", THE TV AND VCR AT "MR. FIX-IT" EVERYTHING WORKS PERFECTLY

LET ME GET THIS STRAIGHT, EL..., YOU GAVE YOUR REC-ROOM FURNITURE TO MIKE AND DEANNA—AND BOUGHT SECOND HAND STUFF FOR YOURSELF?

CLICK!

I'VE ALWAYS SACRIFICED FOR MY CHILDREN CONNIE—BUT, I'VE NEVER HAD THIS MUCH FUN DOING IT!

SO, YOU'RE NICELY SETTLED INTO YOUR NEW APARTMENT, ARE YOU?—THAT'S GREAT, SON!

NO, WE'RE GLAD YOU TOOK OUR REC ROOM FURNITURE. YOUR MOM HAS ALREADY REPLACED EVERYTHING....AND, SHE BOUGHT IT ALL SECOND HAND!

SHE CHECKED ADS IN THE PAPER, SEARCHED THROUGH THE THRIFT SHOPS AND HAD AN ABSOLUTELY WONDERFUL TIME!—WHICH IS WHY I'M CALLING...

.....DO YOU NEED ANY MORE STUFF?

PUNCH
PUNCH
PUNCH
PUNCH

FLOSS
FLOSS
FLOSS

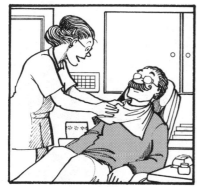

THE DOCTOR WILL BE WITH YOU IN A MINUTE MR. VOLOSATI.

SNORKL

IN THE MEANTIME, IF YOU NEED ANYTHING, NANCY WILL BE ASSISTING US TODAY.

SNRK

YOU'RE HAVING TROUBLE BREATHING? —JUST LET ME CUT SOME OF THAT RUBBER SHIELD AWAY

GRMBRGH! GNO! FNST BRGHL! ARG!

AAAUGHHH!!

NOBODY TOLD ME HE HAD A MOUSTACHE!

GRANDPA, ARE YOU GOING TO SELL POPPIES FOR REMEMBRANCE DAY?

YES, DEAR.

COULD I BUY ONE?

OF COURSE!

VICTIMS & VETERANS OF WAR
LEST WE FORGET

THAT WAS A GREAT MEAL, RUBY!

NO PROBLEM. I LIKE HAVING YOU HERE.

WANNA STICK AROUND FOR A WHILE?

I'VE GOT READING TO DO, CANDACE— AND THERE'S WORK DUE TOMORROW

I KNOW... I'M GLAD I DECIDED TO GO BACK TO SCHOOL IN JANUARY. AT LEAST I'LL BE ABLE TO PICK UP A COUPLE OF CREDITS.

HEY, DON'T APOLOGIZE FOR TAKING TIME OFF. AT LEAST YOU MADE A DECISION.

AND YOU SURE GET CREDIT FOR THAT!!

I'D BETTER HIT THE ROAD TOO, BABE. I'LL WALK WITH LIZ BACK TO THE APARTMENT.

SEE YOU, RUDY!

I THINK IT'S FUN THAT CANDACE LIVES WITH HER AUNT RUBY, AND IS DATING A GUY CALLED "RUDY"!

SO, I SHOULD GO BY THE NAME "RUDOLPH"?

RUDOLPH IS A GOOD NAME. IT'S A CLASSIC, ARISTOCRATIC EUROPEAN NAME!—WHAT'S WRONG WITH "RUDOLPH"?

ASK ME IN DECEMBER.

THANKS FOR WALKING ME BACK TO THE APARTMENT. I'M NOT CRAZY ABOUT BEING OUT ALONE AT NIGHT.

ME NEITHER!

SEEMS WIERD NOT TO BE LIVING HERE ANYMORE.

SORRY YOU HAD TO MOVE OUT.

IT'S NOT YOUR FAULT, LIZ. BESIDES, I'M JUST DOWN THE HALL—AN' I'VE GOT MY OWN PRIVATE SPACE NOW!

SEE? IT'S PERFECT!—BIG CLOSET, TWO WINDOWS— WHAT MORE DO I NEED?

FURNITURE WOULD BE NICE.

I'M NOT OBSESSED BY MATERIAL THINGS, LIZ. I CAN SLEEP ON AN AIR MATTRESS, USE A BOX FOR A BEDSIDE TABLE....

TROUBLE WITH FURNITURE IS- YOU GOTTA **MOVE** IT! THE WAY I LIVE, I CAN PACK UP IN AN HOUR, AND BE GONE!

I AM SO DIFFERENT FROM ERIC, MAN. HE'S GOTTA HAVE THINGS. IF HE SEES SOMETHING HE WANTS, HE GOES AFTER IT. AN' HE USUALLY GETS IT!

FOR EXAMPLE?

...HE'S LIVING WITH YOU, ISN'T HE?!

ERIC TOLD ME WHEN HE SAW YOU ON CAMPUS, HE'D BE DATING YOU WITHIN A WEEK!

OH, REALLY.

SO WHAT AM I, RUDY? -A COMPANION OR A CONQUEST? DOES ERIC LOVE ME, OR AM I JUST "NICE TO HAVE AROUND"?

CHEEZE! DON'T ASK ME STUFF LIKE THAT!!!

WHERE DOES HE GO WHEN HE'S OUT WITH HIS "FRIENDS"? IS HE SEEING SOMEONE ELSE?! -TELL ME IS HE SEEING SOMEONE?!

RIGHT NOW, LIZ... IT APPEARS THAT I'M SEEING YOU!

HEY, ERIC! HOW'S IT GOING?

WHAT'S ELIZABETH DOING HERE, RUDY?

NOTHING!

HE WALKED ME HOME FROM CANDACE'S PLACE- AND, I WANTED TO SEE HIS NEW APARTMENT.

WE WERE JUST TALKING

OH.

OK. I'LL BUY THAT! IF YOU SAY NOTHING'S GOING ON, I BELIEVE YOU! I ACCEPT YOUR WORD, RIGHT? I'M BEING TOTALLY TRUSTING!

AND YOU TRUST ME TOO, DON'T YOU, LIZ? I WANT TO HEAR YOU SAY IT!

I TRUST YOU ERIC! -OF COURSE I DO!!

INTERESTING.... I ALWAYS WONDERED WHY CREEPS WE'RE SO SUCCESSFUL.

WRITE, WRITE, WRITE, WRITE, WRITE...

TYPE, TYPE, TYPE, TYPE...

STUDY, STUDY, STUDY, STUDY...

YOU GOTTA BE KIDDING.

PARTY PARTY PARTY

TON AT WA

Lynn

WHERE'S ERIC TONIGHT, LIZ?

VISITING HIS MOTHER.

HE SAID SHE'S BEEN BUGGING HIM TO COME AND SEE HER, SO HE FINALLY GAVE IN, AN' WENT FOR SUPPER.

...YEAH?

WELL, I HOPE HE MAKES IT BACK IN TIME FOR HIS EXAM TOMORROW.

WHAT DO YOU MEAN?

HIS MOM'S IN MONTREAL FOR TWO WEEKS.

Lynn

ERIC WOULDN'T LIE TO ME. WHY WOULD HE SAY HE WAS VISITING HIS MOTHER'S IF HE WASN'T?!

ALL I KNOW IS, SHE'S IN MONTREAL, AN' THAT'S A 6 HOUR DRIVE FROM HERE.

YOU MEAN, HE LIED TO ME?

ELIZABETH, OPEN YOUR EYES. WHAT ARE YOU STUDYING RIGHT NOW?

PSYCHOLOGY AND WOMENS' ISSUES

AND?....

I KNOW WHAT YOU'RE GETTING AT, RUDY... BUT THAT ABUSIVE STUFF DOESN'T APPLY TO **ME**!!

Lynn

HEY, CANDACE, WANNA GRAB A COFFEE SOMEPLACE?

SURE. I'LL TELL MY AUNT I'LL BE BACK IN AN HOUR.

YOU LOOK GRUESOME. WHAT'S UP?

OH, MAN...

I THINK ERIC'S SEEING SOMEONE ELSE. DO YOU KNOW ANYTHING?

THIS IS, LIKE THE WORST MESS. RUDY TOLD ME HE MOVED OUT OF YOUR APARTMENT BECAUSE OF THE WAY ERIC WAS TREATING YOU.

REALLY?

.... I THOUGHT HE MOVED OUT BECAUSE OF THE WAY I WAS TREATING **HIM**!

YOU GOTTA KNOW THAT ERIC'S FOOLING AROUND ON YOU, LIZ.

DON'T SAY THAT.

HE'S ALSO TOTALLY MANIPULATIVE! HE WOULDN'T EVEN LET YOU GO HOME FOR THANKSGIVING!

HE WANTED ME TO MEET HIS MOM! SHE'S A NICE WOMAN.

YOU BELIEVE EVERYTHING HE TELLS YOU!

HE ALWAYS HAS GOOD REASONS FOR THE THINGS HE DOES, CANDACE – AND, I LOVE HIM! I REALLY LOVE HIM!!!

THEN, YOU HAVE TO ASK YOURSELF ..."DOES BEING IN LOVE MEAN I HAVE TO PUT UP WITH *@★Ø*?!!"

ERIC'S A GOOD LOOKING GUY, LIZ. I WAS REALLY JEALOUS WHEN HE ASKED ME TO INTRODUCE YOU TO HIM.

YOU WERE?

THEN I MET RUDY. HE'S NO PIECE OF CALENDAR ART, BUT HE TREATS ME LIKE GOLD!

HE CALLS BEFORE HE COMES OVER, HE'S ALWAYS ON TIME. HE'S POLITE AND THOUGHTFUL AND HONEST AND KIND.

WOW.

YEAH! I STARTED TO THINK THERE WAS SOMETHING **WRONG** WITH HIM!

I'M GLAD YOU AN' RUDY ARE GETTING ALONG SO WELL CANDACE

Coffee Bar

YEAH... IT'S RARE.

I'M SO USED TO BEING DUMPED ON ... I JUST FIGURED THAT'S THE WAY LIFE WAS.

THAT'S WHY I NEVER SERIOUSLY HOOKED UP WITH ANYONE. IF YOU'RE GONNA END UP IN THE EX-FILES, WHY INVEST YOUR EMOTIONS, RIGHT?

NOW, I'M THINKING— LOVE IS WHEN SOMEONE TREATS YOU THE WAY YOU WANT TO BE TREATED.... WITH RESPECT! LIKE, YOU MEAN SOMETHING!

YOU DESERVE SOMEONE BETTER THAN ERIC, LIZ.

MAYBE HE'LL CHANGE!

STUDY, STUDY, STUDY READ, STUDY, READ STUDYYY...SNORRGHH

PLOP!

SNOZ ZZZZzz

SNAP!!

UH?

?

WHOA! WHAT'S THIS?

I JUST THOUGHT I'D COOK TONIGHT

CHECK OUT THE AMBIANCE. I EVEN BOUGHT THE BEST CHEAP WINE I COULD AFFORD

IT LOOKS REAL GOOD, LIZ!

YOU ARE SO PRETTY. I LOVE THE WAY THE CANDLE LIGHT RE-FLECTS IN YOUR BIG BLUE EYES!

I KNEW IT!

EVERYONE THINKS ERIC'S BEING MEAN TO ME!

BUT, THEY'RE ALL WRONG!

143